HTML

Introductory Concepts and Techniques

THIRD EDITION

Gary B. Shelly
Thomas J. Cashman
Denise M. Woods

THOMSON
COURSE TECHNOLOGY

COURSE TECHNOLOGY
25 THOMSON PLACE
BOSTON MA 02210

SHELLY
CASHMAN
SERIES®

Australia • Canada • Denmark • Japan • Mexico • New Zealand • Philippines • Puerto Rico • Singapore
South Africa • Spain • United Kingdom • United States

HTML Introductory Concepts and Techniques, Third Edition

Gary B. Shelly
Thomas J. Cashman
Denise M. Woods

Executive Director:
Cheryl Costantini

Senior Acquisitions Editor:
Dana Merk

Senior Editor:
Alexandra Arnold

Editorial Assistant:
Selena Coppock

Series Consulting Editor:
Jim Quasney

Print Buyer:
Laura Burns

Production Editor:
Jennifer Goguen

Development Editor:
Lisa Strite

Copy Editor:
Nancy Lamm

Proofreader:
Lori Silfen

Cover Image:
John Still

Compositor:
GEX Publishing Services

Indexer:
Cristina Haley

Printer:
Banta Menasha

Introductory Concepts and Techniques
THIRD EDITION

Contents

Project Four

Creating Tables in a Web Site

Appendix A

HTML Quick Reference

Appendix B

Browser-Safe Color Palette

Preface

The Shelly Cashman Series® offers the finest textbooks in computer education. We are proud of the fact that our previous HTML books have been so well received. With each new edition of our HTML books, we have made significant improvements based on the comments made by instructors and students. The *HTML, Third Edition* books continue with the innovation, quality, and reliability you have come to expect from the Shelly Cashman Series.

In this HTML book, you will find an educationally sound, highly visual, and easy-to-follow pedagogy that combines a vastly improved step-by-step approach with corresponding screens. All projects and exercises in this book are designed to take advantage of enhancements to HTML and XHTML standard. The popular More About feature offers in-depth knowledge of HTML. The new Q&A feature offers students a way to solidify important HTML concepts. The Learn It Online page presents a wealth of additional exercises to ensure your students have all the reinforcement they need. The project material is developed to ensure that students will see the importance of learning HTML for future coursework.

Objectives of This Textbook

HTML: Introductory Concepts and Techniques, Third Edition is intended for use in combination with other books in an introductory course on creating Web pages. This book also is suitable for use as a stand alone in a one-credit hour course or a continuing education course. No experience with Web page development or computer programming is required. Specific objectives of this book are as follows:

- To teach the fundamentals of developing Web pages
- To acquaint students with the HTML language and creating Web pages suitable for course work, professional purposes, and personal use
- To expose students to common Web page formats and functions
- To promote curiosity and independent exploration of World Wide Web resources
- To develop an exercise-oriented approach that allows students to learn by example
- To encourage independent study and help those who are learning how to create Web pages in a distance education environment

The Shelly Cashman Approach

Features of the Shelly Cashman Series *HTML, Third Edition* books include:

- **Project Orientation:** Each project in the book presents a practical problem and complete solution using an easy-to-understand methodology.
- **Step-by-Step, Screen-by-Screen Instructions:** Each of the tasks required to complete a project is identified throughout the project. Full-color screens accompany the steps.
- **Thoroughly Tested Projects:** Unparalleled quality is ensured because every screen in the book is produced by the author only after performing a step, and then each project must pass Course Technology's award-winning Quality Assurance program.
- **More About and Q&A Features:** These marginal annotations provide background information, tips, and answers to common questions that complement the topics covered, adding depth and perspective to the learning process.

More About

Linking Colors

You can change the link colors in popular browsers. In Microsoft Internet Explorer, you find color selection on the Tools menu using Internet Options. In Netscape Communicator, click Preferences on the Edit menu. In both products, you change colors by clicking the color bars.

Q: What are browser-safe colors and why should they be used?

A: The browser limits the colors that a user can see on a Web page to 216 colors. Because a browser can display these colors correctly, they are called browser-safe colors. To ensure that the majority of your users can see Web page colors as intended, Web developers should use only browser-safe colors when designing Web pages. Appendix B provides a list of the 216 browser-safe colors that can be used without worry.

● Integration of the World Wide Web: The World Wide Web is integrated into the HTML learning experience by (1) More About annotations that send students to Web sites for up-to-date information and alternative approaches to tasks; (2) an HTML Quick Reference Summary Web page that summarizes HTML tags and attibutes; and (3) the Learn It Online page at the end of each project, which has project reinforcement exercises, learning games, and other types of student activities.

Organization of This Textbook

HTML: Introductory Concepts and Techniques, Third Edition is comprised of four projects and two appendices. Each project ends with a large number of exercises to reinforce what students learn in the project. The projects and appendices are organized as follows:

Project 1 - Introduction to HTML This introductory project provides students with an overview of the Internet, World Wide Web, Web pages, HTML, and Web development. Topics include the types and purposes of Web sites; Web browsers; HTML standards; Dynamic Hypertext Markup Language (DHTML) and Extensible Hypertext Markup Language (XHTML) and their relationship to HTML. Additionally, Web editors, the five phases of the Web development life cycle, and the importance of usability testing are defined.

Project 2 - Creating and Editing a Web Page In Project 2, students are introduced to basic HTML tags and the various parts of a Web page. Topics include starting and quitting Notepad and a browser; entering headings and text into an HTML file; creating a bulleted list with HTML; adding background color, a horizontal rule, and an image; saving the HTML file and viewing it in the browser; printing the HTML file and the Web page; and Web page design.

Project 3 - Creating Web pages with Links, Images, and Formatted Text In Project 3, students are introduced to linking terms and definitions. Topics include adding an e-mail link; linking to another page on the same Web site; linking to another Web site; setting link targets within a page; linking to targets; types of image files; alternative text for images; defining image size; wrapping text around an image; and inserting images onto Web pages.

Project 4 - Creating Tables in a Web Site In Project 4, students learn how to create tables using HTML tags. First, students assess table needs and then plan the table. Topics include table definitions and terms; table uses; creating borderless tables; inserting images into tables; vertical and horizontal alignment within a table; adding color to a cell; adding links to another page; adding an e-mail link; using the rowspan and colspan attributes; adding captions; and spacing within and between cells.

Appendix A – HTML Quick Reference Appendix A includes an HTML quick reference that contains the most frequently used tags and their associated attributes.

Appendix B – Browser-Safe Color Palette Appendix B summarizes the 216 browser-safe colors that display equally well on different monitors, operating systems, and browsers – including both the Windows and Mac OS operating systems and Internet Explorer and Netscape browsers.

End-of-Project Student Activities

A notable strength of the Shelly Cashman Series *HTML* books is the extensive student activities at the end of each project. Well-structured student activities can make the difference between students merely participating in a class and students retaining the information they learn. The activities in the Shelly Cashman Series *HTML* books include the following.

- **What You Should Know** A listing of the tasks completed within a project together with the pages on which the step-by-step, screen-by-screen explanations appear.
- **Learn It Online** Every project features a Learn It Online page that contains 12 exercises. These exercises include True/False, Multiple Choice, Short Answer, Flash Cards, Practice Test, Learning Games, Tips and Tricks, Newsgroup usage, Expanding Your Horizons, Search Sleuth, and Online Help.
- **Apply Your Knowledge** This exercise usually requires students to open and manipulate a file on the Data Disk that parallels the activities learned in the project. To obtain a copy of the Data Disk, follow the instructions on the inside back cover of this textbook.
- **In the Lab** Three in-depth assignments per project require students to utilize the project concepts and techniques to solve problems on a computer.
- **Cases and Places** Five unique real-world case-study situations, including one small-group activity.

Instructor Resources CD-ROM

The Shelly Cashman Series is dedicated to providing you with all of the tools you need to make your class a success. Information on all supplementary materials is available through your Course Technology representative or by calling one of the following telephone numbers: Colleges and Universities, 1-800-648-7450; High Schools, 1-800-824-5179; Private Career Colleges, 1-800-347-7707; Canada, 1-800-268-2222; Corporations with IT Training Centers, 1-800-648-7450; and Government Agencies, Health-Care Organizations, and Correctional Facilities, 1-800-477-3692.

The Instructor Resources for this textbook include both teaching and testing aids. The contents of each item on the Instructor Resources CD-ROM (ISBN 0-619-25520-X) are described below.

INSTRUCTOR'S MANUAL The Instructor's Manual is made up of Microsoft Word files, which include detailed lesson plans with page number references, lecture notes, teaching tips, classroom activities, discussion topics, projects to assign, and transparency references. The transparencies are available through the Figure Files described on the next page.

LECTURE SUCCESS SYSTEM The Lecture Success System consists of intermediate files that correspond to certain figures in the book, allowing you to step through the creation of an application in a project during a lecture without entering large amounts of data.

SYLLABUS Sample syllabi, which can be customized easily to a course, are included. The syllabi cover policies, class and lab assignments and exams, and procedural information.

FIGURE FILES Illustrations for every figure in the textbook are available in electronic form. Use this ancillary to present a slide show in lecture or to print transparencies for use in lecture with an overhead projector. If you have a personal computer and LCD device, this ancillary can be an effective tool for presenting lectures.

POWERPOINT PRESENTATIONS PowerPoint Presentations is a multimedia lecture presentation system that provides slides for each project. Presentations are based on project objectives. Use this presentation system to present well-organized lectures that are both interesting and knowledge based. PowerPoint Presentations provides consistent coverage at schools that use multiple lecturers.

SOLUTIONS TO EXERCISES Solutions are included for the end-of-project exercises, as well as the Project Reinforcement exercises.

TEST BANK & TEST ENGINE The ExamView test bank includes 110 questions for every project (25 multiple choice, 50 true/false, and 35 short answer) with page number references and, when appropriate, figure references. A version of the test bank you can print also is included. The test bank comes with a copy of the test engine, ExamView, the ultimate tool for your objective-based testing needs. ExamView is a state-of-the-art test builder that is easy to use. ExamView enables you to create paper-, LAN-, or Web-based tests from test banks designed specifically for your Course Technology textbook. Utilize the ultra-efficient QuickTest Wizard to create tests in less than five minutes by taking advantage of Course Technology's question banks, or customize your own exams from scratch.

DATA FILES FOR STUDENTS All the files that are required by students to complete the exercises are included. You can distribute the files on the Instructor Resources CD-ROM to your students over a network, or you can have them follow the instructions on the inside back cover of this book to obtain a copy of the Data Disk.

ADDITIONAL ACTIVITIES FOR STUDENTS These additional activities consist of Project Reinforcement Exercises, which are true/false, multiple choice, and short answer questions that help students gain confidence in the material learned.

Online Content

Course Technology offers textbook-based content for Blackboard, WebCT, and MyCourse 2.1.

BLACKBOARD AND WEBCT As the leading provider of IT content for the Blackboard and WebCT platforms, Course Technology delivers rich content that enhances your textbook to give your students a unique learning experience.

MYCOURSE 2.1 MyCourse 2.1 is Course Technology's powerful online course management and content delivery system. MyCourse 2.1 allows nontechnical users to create, customize, and deliver Web-based courses; post content and assignments; manage student enrollment; administer exams; track results in the online grade book; and more.

www.blackboard.com

Introduction to HTML

CASE PERSPECTIVE

Shomir Kini has been selected as the project leader for the company's Web development effort. This project includes the development of a corporate Internet site that displays information about the company to prospective customers and a corporate intranet that displays information about the company to employees. In order for this to be a successful project, Shomir formed a development team that included people from several functional areas of the company, including the Human Resources, Marketing, Finance, and Engineering departments. You represented the Information Technology (IT) department at the kick-off meeting. Shomir was very concerned about the lack of Internet knowledge from the employees who represented their functional areas. The majority of questions appeared to be the result of employees not understanding the main concepts behind Internet and Hypertext Markup Language (HTML) technology. You suggested that Shomir work with you to develop a seminar on Internet and HTML basics that he can present to the development team. In this seminar, you want to describe the Internet, the World Wide Web, and intranets. You want to discuss Web browsers, definitions of HTML and the associated key terms, the five phases of the Web development life cycle, and what role each team member will play in the Web development effort.

Introduction to HTML

Objectives

You will have mastered the material in this project when you can:

- Describe the Internet and its associated key terms
- Describe the World Wide Web and its associated key terms
- Identify the types and purposes of Web sites
- Discuss Web browsers and identify their purpose
- Define Hypertext Markup Language (HTML) and the standards used for Web development
- Define Dynamic Hypertext Markup Language (DHTML) and describe its relationship to HTML
- Define Extensible Hypertext Markup Language (XHTML) and describe its relationship to HTML
- Describe tools used to create HTML documents
- Discuss the five phases of the Web development life cycle
- Describe Web site structures and the purpose of each structure
- Describe the importance of testing throughout the Web development life cycle

Introduction

Each day, you make decisions in all areas of your life. Having quick access to information to help you make good, informed decisions is vitally important. Today, computers and networks allow people to gather, analyze, and use information to make decisions and to communicate with others around the world. The world's largest network is the Internet — a worldwide network of computers that houses information on a multitude of subjects.

What Is the Internet?

The **Internet** is a worldwide collection of computer networks that links together millions of computers used by businesses, the government, educational institutions, organizations, and individuals using modems, telephone lines, television cables, and other communications devices and media (Figure 1-1). A **network** is a group of two or more computers that are connected together to share resources and information. Today, high-, medium-, and low-speed data lines connect networks. These data lines allow data to move from one computer to another. The **Internet backbone** is a collection of high-speed data lines that connect major computer systems located around the world. An

FIGURE 1-1 The Internet is a worldwide collection of computer networks.

Internet service provider (**ISP**) is a company that has a permanent connection to the Internet backbone. ISPs utilize high- or medium-speed data lines to allow individuals and companies to connect to the backbone for access to the Internet. A consumer's Internet connection at home generally is a low-speed data line that connects to the ISP.

More than 650 million people in 240 countries connect to the Internet using computers in their homes, offices, schools, and public locations such as libraries. Users with computers connected to the Internet can access a variety of services, including e-mail, newsgroups, and the World Wide Web (Figure 1-2).

FIGURE 1-2 The Internet makes available a variety of services such as e-mail, newsgroups, and the World Wide Web.

More About

Internet and WWW History

Many Web sites are dedicated to telling the story of the creation of the Internet and the World Wide Web. The World Wide Web Consortium (W3C), the de facto organization to govern HTML, provides a rich history of the Internet and the World Wide Web. To view their history, visit the HTML More About Web page (scsite.com/html3e/more) and then click History.

What Is the World Wide Web?

The **World Wide Web**, also called the **Web**, is the part of the Internet that supports multimedia and consists of a collection of linked documents. To support multimedia, the Web relies on the **Hypertext Transfer Protocol** (**HTTP**), which is a set of rules for exchanging text, graphic, sound, video, and other multimedia files. The linked documents, or pages of information, on the Web are known as **Web pages**. Because the Web supports multimedia, text, graphics, sound, and video, a Web page can include any of these elements.

A **Web site** is a related collection of Web pages that is created and maintained by an individual, company, educational institution, or other organization. For example, as shown in Figure 1-3, many colleges and universities, such as Arizona State University, publish and maintain Web sites. Each Web site contains a **home page**, which is the first document users see when they access the Web site. The home page often serves as an index or table of contents to other documents and files stored on the site.

university home page

FIGURE 1-3   A Web site is a related collection of Web pages that is created and maintained by an individual, company, educational institution, or other organization.

Web Servers

Web pages are stored on a **Web server**, or **host**, which is a computer that stores and sends (serves) requested Web pages and other files. Any computer that has Web server software installed and is connected to the Internet can act as a Web server. Every Web site is stored on, and runs from, one or more Web servers. A very large Web site may be spread over a number of servers in different geographic locations.

Publishing is copying Web pages and other files to a Web server. Once a Web page is published, anyone who has access to the Internet can view it, regardless of where the Web server is located. For example, although the Arizona State University Web site is stored on a Web server in Tempe, Arizona, it is available for viewing by anyone in the world.

Web Site Types and Purposes

The three general types of Web sites are Internet, intranet, and extranet. Table 1-1 lists characteristics of each of these three types of Web sites.

Table 1-1	Types of Web Sites		
TYPE	USERS	ACCESS	APPLICATIONS
Internet	Anyone	Public	Share information (personal information, product catalogs, classroom information, etc.) with the public
Intranet	Employees or members of organization	Private	Share information (forms, manuals, schedules, etc.) with employees or members
Extranet	Select business partners or customers	Private	Share information (inventory updates, product specifications, financial information, etc.) with partners and customers

An **Internet site,** also known as a Web site, is a site generally available to the public. Individuals, groups, companies, and educational institutions use Internet sites, or Web sites, for a variety of purposes. An individual, for example, might create a personal Web site that includes his or her résumé to make it easily accessible to any interested employers. Another personal Web site might present information about a person's hobbies or interests. Families also can share photographs of special events, schedules, or other information with each other via Web sites (Figure 1-4).

FIGURE 1-4 Web page on a personal Web site.

More About

E-Commerce

Today, e-commerce is a standard part of doing business. E-commerce technologies, however, continue to change, offering new applications and potential uses. Several online magazines are dedicated to providing an in depth look at e-commerce. To learn more about e-commerce, visit the HTML More About Web page (scsite.com/html3e/more) and then click E-commerce.

Companies use Web sites to advertise or sell their products and services worldwide, as well as to provide technical and product support for their customers. Many company Web sites also support **electronic commerce** (**e-commerce**), which is the buying and selling of goods and services on the Internet. Using e-commerce technologies, these Web sites allow customers to browse product catalogs, comparison shop, and order products online. Many company Web sites also provide job postings and announcements, a frequently asked questions (FAQs) section, customer feedback links to solicit comments from their customers, and searchable technical support databases.

Colleges, universities, and other schools use Web sites to distribute information about areas of study, provide course information, or register students for classes online. Instructors use their Web sites to issue announcements, post questions on the reading material, list contact information, and provide easy access to their lecture notes and slides, as shown in Figure 1-5.

FIGURE 1-5 Web page from a university's Web site.

More About

Intranets and Extranets

The CIO Intranet/Extranet Research Center provides valuable information on building and maintaining an intranet or extranet, along with additional resources. To view their Web site, visit the HTML More About Web page (scsite.com/html3e/more) and then click Intranets/Extranets.

An **intranet** is a private network that uses standard Internet technologies to share company information among employees. An intranet is contained within a company or organization's network; some intranets also are password-protected to provide additional security. Policy and procedure manuals usually are found on an intranet, in addition to a variety of forms. Other documents, such as employee directories, company newsletters, product catalogs, and training manuals, often are distributed via an intranet. An intranet also can be used to facilitate working in groups and collecting feedback from employees.

An **extranet** is a private network that uses Internet technologies to share business information with select corporate partners or key customers. Most extranets are password-protected to restrict access to specific suppliers, vendors, partners, or customers. Companies and organizations can use an extranet to share product manuals, training modules, inventory status, and order information. An extranet also might support e-commerce to allow retailers to purchase inventory directly or to pay bills online, which is more efficient than calling partners to check on inventory levels or account status.

Web Browsers

In order to view a Web page on any type of Web site, a computer needs to have a Web browser installed. A **Web browser**, also called a **browser**, is a program that interprets and displays Web pages and enables you to view and interact with a Web page. The two more popular browsers in use today are Microsoft Internet Explorer and Netscape Navigator. Browsers provide a variety of features, including the capability to locate Web pages, to move forward and backward between Web pages, to bookmark favorite Web pages, and to choose security settings.

To locate a Web page using a browser, you type its Uniform Resource Locator (URL) in the browser's Address, or Location, bar. A **Uniform Resource Locator** (**URL**) is the address of a document or other file accessible on the Internet. An example of a URL on the Web is:

http://www.scsite.com/html3e/index.htm

The URL indicates to the browser to use the Hypertext Transfer Protocol (http) to locate a Web page named index.htm in the html3e folder on a Web server named scsite.com. Web page URLs can be found in a wide range of places, including school catalogs, business cards, product packaging, and advertisements.

Hyperlinks are used to link one Web page to other Web pages. A **hyperlink**, also called a **link**, is an element used to connect one Web page to another Web page on the same, or a different, Web server located anywhere in the world. Clicking a hyperlink allows you to move quickly from one Web page to another. You also can click hyperlinks to move to a different section of the same Web page.

Hyperlinks are an essential part of the World Wide Web. With hyperlinks, a Web site user does not have to view information linearly. Instead, he or she can choose to click the available hyperlinks in order to view the information in a variety of ways. Many different Web page elements, including text, graphics, and animations, can serve as hyperlinks. Figure 1-6 on the next page shows examples of several different Web page elements used as hyperlinks.

What Is Hypertext Markup Language?

Web pages are created using **Hypertext Markup Language** (**HTML**), which is the authoring language used to create documents on the World Wide Web. HTML uses a set of special instructions called **tags** or **markup** to define the structure and layout of a Web document and specify how the page is displayed in a browser.

A Web page is a file that contains both text and HTML tags. HTML tags *mark* the text to define how it displays when viewed as a page on the Web. HTML includes hundreds of tags used to format Web pages and create hyperlinks to other documents or Web pages. For instance, the HTML tags <strong> and </strong> are used to indicate bold text, <p> and </p> are used to indicate a new paragraph, and <hr /> is used to display a horizontal rule across the page. Figure 1-7a on the next page shows the HTML tags needed to create the Web page shown in Figure 1-7b.

Q & A

Q: What are browser-safe colors and why should they be used?

A: The browser limits the colors that a user can see on a Web page to 216 colors. Because a browser can display these colors correctly, they are called browser-safe colors. To ensure that the majority of your users can see Web page colors as intended, Web developers should use only browser-safe colors when designing Web pages. Appendix B provides a list of the 216 browser-safe colors that can be used without worry.

FIGURE 1-6 A Web page can use several different Web page elements as hyperlinks.

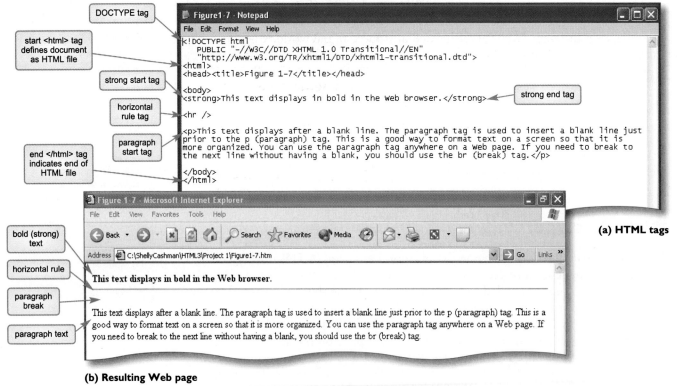

(a) HTML tags

(b) Resulting Web page

FIGURE 1-7 A Web page is a file that contains both text and HTML tags.

HTML is **platform independent**, meaning you can create, or *code*, an HTML file on one type of computer and then use a browser on another type of computer to view that file as a Web page.

HTML History

In 1989, Tim Berners-Lee and Robert Calliau set out to improve their process for handling hundreds of research documents. Over the next two years, Berners-Lee developed a collection of tags that described how a document should look when viewed in a browser. For example, the tags defined text displayed as a header, in a paragraph, or as regular text. In addition, these tags made it possible to create hyperlinks to connect documents together. Berners-Lee's system of tags became known as HTML and created the use of hyperlinks that now define the World Wide Web.

In 1994, Tim Berners-Lee founded the World Wide Web Consortium in an effort to encourage the universality and interoperability of HTML and to promote an open forum for discussion among Web developers. The **World Wide Web Consortium** (**W3C**) is an industry consortium that seeks to promote standards for the evolution of the Web and Web technologies. Although no one organization dictates the rules or standards for HTML, the W3C is regarded as the de facto organization to govern HTML.

In addition to information about HTML standards, the W3C Web site (w3.org) also includes information about accessibility, privacy, internationalization, and new Web development languages and techniques (Figure 1-8). Membership in the W3C is open to all types of organizations, including educational, government, and commercial entities. Members generally include technology vendors, content providers, corporations, research laboratories, standards bodies, and governments, all of which help to ensure the strength and direction of the consortium.

FIGURE 1-8 W3C Web site home page.

HTML Elements

HTML is a subset of Standard Generalized Markup Language (SGML), which is a standard for how to organize and tag elements of a document. SGML itself does not specify any particular formatting; rather, it specifies the rules for tagging elements. Government agencies and publishers use SGML to create books and reference documentation.

HTML combines the descriptive tags of SGML with special tags that denote formatting styles for how a document should display in a Web browser. HTML elements include headings, paragraphs, hyperlinks, lists, images, and more. Most HTML elements consist of three parts: a start tag, content, and an end tag. For example, to specify that text should display in bold on a Web page, you would enter the following HTML code:

```
<strong>sample text</strong>
```

where <strong> is the start tag, sample text is the content that will display in bold, and </strong> is the end tag. Table 1-2 shows examples of some HTML elements.

Table 1-2 HTML Elements		
HTML ELEMENT	**HTML TAGS**	**PURPOSE**
Title	<title>...</title>	Indicates title to display on the title bar on the Web page
Body	<body>...</body>	Specifies what displays on the Web page; all Web page content is inserted within the start <body> tag and end </body> tag
Paragraph	<p>...</p>	Inserts a blank line before paragraph text
Line Break	 	Inserts a line break before next element (no blank line)

HTML Coding Practices

Similar to all programming languages, HTML has a set of coding practices designed to simplify the process of creating and editing HTML files and to ensure the Web pages display correctly in different browsers.

When creating an HTML file, you should separate sections of the HTML code with spaces. Adding spaces between sections gives you an immediate view of the sections of code that relate to one another and helps you view the HTML elements in your document more clearly. HTML browsers ignore spaces that exist between the tags in your HTML document, so the spaces inserted within the code will not display on the Web page. Figure 1-9 shows an example of an HTML file, with code sections separated by space lines. Another developer looking at this code can see immediately where the table (lines 9 through 18) and bulleted list (lines 20 through 23) are located in the code.

HTML Versions

HTML has gone through several versions, each of which expands the capabilities of HTML. The most recent version of HTML is HTML 4.01, although most browsers still support the previous HTML versions 3.2 and 2.0. To ensure that browsers can interpret each new version of HTML, the W3C maintains HTML standards, or specifications, which it makes publicly available on its Web site.

FIGURE 1-9 Adding spaces to HTML code separates sections to make reading easier.

Dynamic HTML (DHTML)

HTML can be used with other Web technologies to provide additional Web page functionality. For example, **Dynamic HTML** (**DHTML**) is a term that describes a combination of HTML tags, cascading style sheets (CSS), and a scripting language such as JavaScript. DHTML allows users to create interactive, animated Web pages. CSS, JavaScript, and DHTML are covered in later projects in this book.

Extensible Hypertext Markup Language (XHTML)

Extensible Markup Language (**XML**) is a markup language that uses tags to describe the structure and content of a document, not the format. **Extensible Hypertext Markup Language** (**XHTML**) is a reformulation of HTML so it conforms to Extensible Markup Language (XML) rules. As you have learned, HTML uses tags to describe how a document should be displayed in a Web browser. By incorporating HTML and XML, XHTML combines the benefits of the display features of HTML and the stricter coding standards required by XML.

If you create a Web page in HTML and do not follow HTML coding standards exactly (for example, by not using an end </p> tag), the Web browser on your computer still can interpret and display the Web page correctly. Newer types of browsers, such as those for mobile phones or handheld computers, are not able to interpret HTML code that does not meet the HTML standards. Because XHTML has such strict coding standards, it helps ensure that Web pages created in XHTML will be readable by many different types of applications.

Table 1-3 on the next page lists some of the XHTML coding rules that Web developers should follow to ensure that their HTML code conforms to XHTML standards. All of the projects in this book follow XHTML standards and adhere to the rules outlined in Table 1-3. The specifics of each rule will be explained in detail as it is used in a project.

Table 1-3 XHTML Coding Practices

PRACTICE	INVALID EXAMPLE	VALID EXAMPLE
HTML file must include a DOCTYPE statement	<html> <head><title>sample Web page</title>	<!DOCTYPE html PUBLIC "-//W3C//DTD XHTML 1.0 Transitional//EN" "http://www.w3.org/TR/xhtml1/ DTD/xhtml1-transitional.dtd"> <html> <head><title>sample Web page</title>
All tags and attributes must be written in lowercase	<TABLE WIDTH="100%">	<table width="100%">
All attribute values must be enclosed by single or double quotes	<table width=100%>	<table width="100%">
All tags must be closed, including tags such as img, hr, br, which do not have end tags	<p>This is a paragraph <hr> <p>This is another paragraph	<p>This is a paragraph</p> <hr /> <p>This is another paragraph</p>
All elements must be nested properly	<p><strong>This is a bold paragraph</p></strong>	<p><strong>This is a bold paragraph</strong></p>

Tools for Creating HTML Documents

You can create Web pages using HTML with a simple text editor, such as Notepad, WordPad, or SimpleText. A **text editor** is a program that allows a user to enter, change, save, and print text, such as HTML. Text editors do not have many advanced features, but they do allow you to develop HTML documents easily. For instance, if you want to mark text to be displayed in italics on a Web page, type the text in the text editor and then surround the text with the start (<em>) and end (</em>) tags as shown in Figure 1-10.

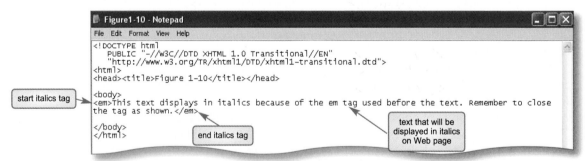

FIGURE 1-10 With a text editor, such as Notepad, you type HTML tags directly in the document.

You also can create Web pages using an HTML editor, such as Macromedia HomeSite or BBEdit. An **HTML editor** is a program that provides basic text-editing functions, as well as more advanced features such as color-coding for various HTML tags, menus to insert HTML tags, and spell checkers.

Many popular software applications also provide features that enable you to develop Web pages easily. Microsoft Word, for example, has a Save as Web Page feature that converts a Word document into an HTML file by automatically adding the HTML tags into the document. Microsoft Excel and Microsoft PowerPoint also have Save as Web Page features. Using Microsoft Access, you can create a Web page that allows you to add, edit, or view data in a database. Each of these applications also provides the capability of inserting hyperlinks, drop-down boxes, option buttons, or scrolling text to the Web page.

These advanced Web features make it simple to save any document, spreadsheet, database, or presentation to display as a Web page. Corporate policy and procedures manuals and PowerPoint presentations, for example, easily can be saved as Web pages and published to the company's intranet site. Extranet users can be given access to Web pages that allow them to view or update information stored in a database.

You also can create Web pages using a WYSIWYG editor, such as Microsoft FrontPage, Macromedia Dreamweaver, or Sausage Software HotDog. A **WYSIWYG editor** is a program that provides a graphical user interface that allows a developer to preview the Web page during its development. WYSIWYG (pronounced *wizzywig*) is an acronym for What You See Is What You Get. A WYSIWYG editor creates the HTML code for you as you add elements to the Web page, which means that you do not have to enter HTML tags directly.

Regardless of which type of program you use to create Web pages, it is important to understand the specifics of HTML so you can make changes outside of the editor. It also is important to understand the Web development life cycle, so the Web pages in your Web site are consistent and complete.

Web Development Life Cycle

In any software development project, a systematic methodology, or process, should be followed through the life cycle of the project to ensure consistency and completeness. The Web development life cycle outlined in this section is one that can be utilized for any size of Web development project. The life cycle includes the following phases: planning, analysis, design and development, testing, and implementation and maintenance. Table 1-4 on the next page lists several questions that should be asked during each phase in the Web development life cycle.

Web Site Planning

Web site planning, which is the first phase of the Web development life cycle, involves identifying the goals or purpose of the Web site. The first step in the Web site planning phase is to answer the question, What is the purpose of this Web site? As you have learned, individuals and groups design and publish Web sites for a variety of purposes. Individuals develop Web sites to share their hobbies, to post résumés, or just to share ideas on personal interests. Organizations create Web sites to keep members informed of upcoming events or to recruit new members. Businesses create Web sites to advertise and sell products or to give their customers 24-hour online support. Instructors publish Web sites to inform students of course policies and requirements. Until you adequately can identify the intended purpose of the Web site, you should not proceed with the Web development project.

In addition to understanding the Web site's purpose, you also should understand who will use the Web site and the computing environments of most of the users. Knowing the makeup of your target audience — including age, gender, general demographic background, and level of computer literacy — will help you design a Web site appropriate for all users. Understanding their computing environments will determine what types of Web technologies to use. For example, if most users had low-speed Internet connections, you would not want to create pages with large graphics or multimedia elements.

More About

Microsoft FrontPage

Microsoft's FrontPage is a popular WYSIWYG editor used by many novice Web developers to create well-designed, interactive Web sites. To get a 30-day trial of the latest version of FrontPage, visit the HTML More About Web page (www.scsite.com/html/more.htm) and click FrontPage.

Table 1-4 Web Development Phases and Questions	
WEB DEVELOPMENT PHASE	**QUESTIONS TO ASK**
Planning	• What is the purpose of this Web site? • Who will use this Web site? • What are the users' computing environments? • Who owns and authors the information on the Web site? • Who decides if/where the information goes on the Web site?
Analysis	• What tasks do the users need to perform? • What information is useful to the users? • What process considerations must be made?
Design and Development	• How will the Web pages be organized? • What type of Web site structure is appropriate for the content? • What forms of multimedia contribute positively to the Web site? • How can accessibility issues be addressed so as not to limit usability? • Do we need to design for an international audience?
Testing	• Is the Web site content correct? • Does the Web site functionality work correctly? • Are users able to find the information they need and to complete desired tasks? • Is the navigation easy to use?
Implementation and Maintenance	• How is the Web site published? • How is the Web site updated? • Who is responsible for content updates? • Who is responsible for structure updates? • How do we notify users about updates to the Web site? • Will the Web site be monitored?

More About

Accessibility Standards

Creating a Web site that is accessible to all users allows your Web site to reach the widest audience. Further, under Section 508 law, any Web site or technology used by a Federal agency must be usable by people with disabilities. To learn more about Section 508 guidelines and how they impact Web page development, visit the HTML More About Web page (scsite.com/html3e/more) and then click Accessibility Standards.

A final aspect to the Web site planning phase is to identify the content owners and authors. To determine this, you need to ask the questions:

• Who owns and authors the information on the Web site?
• Who decides if/where the information goes on the Web site?

Once you have identified who will provide and authorize the Web site content, you can include those individuals in all aspects of the Web development project.

Web Site Analysis

During the analysis phase, you make decisions about the Web site content and functionality. To help define the appropriate Web site content and functionality, you first should identify the tasks that users need to perform. Answering that question allows you to define necessary content to facilitate those tasks and determine useful information for the users. Extraneous content should be eliminated from the Web site, as it does not serve any purpose.

In the analysis phase, it also is important to consider the processes required to support Web site features. For example, if you determine that users should be able to order products via the Web site, then you also need to define the processes or actions to be taken each time an order is submitted. For instance, after an order is submitted, how will that order be processed throughout the back-office business applications, such as inventory control and accounts payable? Will users receive e-mail confirmations with details about their orders?

The analysis phase is one of the more important phases in the Web development life cycle. Clearly, understanding and defining the desired content and functionality of the Web site will direct the type of Web site that you design and reduce changes during Web site development.

Web Site Design and Development

After determining the purpose of the Web site and defining the content and functionality, you need to consider the Web site's design. Some key considerations in Web site design are defining how to organize Web page content, selecting the appropriate Web site structure, determining how to use multimedia, addressing accessibility issues, and designing pages for an international audience.

Many ways to organize a Web page exist, just as many ways to organize a report or paper exist. Table 1-5 lists some organizational standards for creating a Web page that is easy to read and navigate.

Table 1-5 Web Page Organizational Standards		
ELEMENT	**ORGANIZATIONAL STANDARD**	**REASON**
Titles	Use simple titles that clearly explain the purpose of the page	Titles help users understand the purpose of the page; a good title explains the page in the search engine results lists
Headings	Use headings to separate main topics	Headings make a Web page easier to read; simple headlines clearly explain the purpose of the page
Horizontal rules	Insert horizontal rules to separate main topics	Horizontal rules provide graphical elements to break up Web page content
Paragraphs	Use paragraphs to help divide large amounts of text	Paragraphs provide shorter, more-readable sections of text
Lists	Utilize bulleted or numbered lists when appropriate	Lists provide organized, easy-to-read text that readers can scan easily
Page length	Maintain suitable Web page lengths	Web users do not always scroll to view information on longer pages; appropriate page lengths increase likelihood that users view key information
Information	Emphasize the most important information by placing it at the top of a Web page	Web users are quick to peruse a page; placing critical information at the top of the page increases the likelihood that users will view key information
Other	Incorporate a contact e-mail address; include the date of the last modification	E-mail addresses and dates give users a way to contact a Web developer with questions; the date last modified helps users determine the timeliness of site information

Web sites can use any of several different types of structures, including linear, hierarchical, and webbed. Each structure links, or connects, the Web pages in a different way to define how users navigate through the site and view the Web pages. You should select a structure for the Web site based on how users will navigate through the site to complete tasks and view the Web site content.

A **linear** Web site structure connects Web pages in a straight line, as shown in Figure 1-11. A linear Web site structure is appropriate if the information on the Web pages should be read in a specific order. For example, if the information on the first Web page was necessary for understanding information on the second Web page, you

FIGURE 1-11 Linear Web site structure.

More About

User Interface Design

The user interface design is a very important aspect of a Web site. If a site is designed poorly, users may be unable to find the desired information or complete a task, which makes the Web site ineffective. To learn more about good Web design principles, visit the HTML More About Web page (scsite.com/html3e/more) and then click Design.

should use a linear structure. Each page would have links from one Web page to the next, as well as a link back to the home page.

A **hierarchical** Web site structure connects Web pages in a tree-like structure, as shown in Figure 1-12. A hierarchical Web site structure works well on a site with a main index or table of contents page that links to all other Web pages. With this structure, the main index page would display general information and secondary pages would include more detailed information.

A **webbed** Web site structure has no set organization, as shown in Figure 1-13. A webbed Web site structure works best on Web sites with information that does not need to be read in a specific order and with many navigation options users can select. The World Wide Web itself uses a webbed structure, so users can navigate among Web pages in any order they choose.

FIGURE 1-13 Webbed Web site structure.

FIGURE 1-12 Hierarchical Web site structure.

Most Web sites are a combination of the linear, hierarchical, and webbed structures. Some information on the Web site might be organized hierarchically from an index page; other information might be accessible from all areas of the site; while other information might be organized linearly to be read in a specific order. Using a combination of the three structures is appropriate, if it helps users navigate through the site easily.

Regardless of the structure or structures that you use, you should balance the narrowness and depth of the Web site. A **broad Web site** is one in which the home page is the main index page, and all other Web pages are linked individually to the home page (Figure 1-14). By making the other Web pages accessible only through the home page, a broad Web site forces the user to return to the home page in order to move from one Web page to another. The structure makes navigation time-consuming and limiting for users. A better structure would present a user with navigation alternatives that allow for direct movement between the Web pages.

FIGURE 1-14 Broad Web site.

A **deep Web site** is one that has many levels of pages, requiring the user to click many times to reach a particular Web page (Figure 1-15). By requiring a visitor to move through several Web pages before reaching the desired Web page, a deep Web site forces a user to spend time viewing interim pages with little or no content.

As a Web developer, you must select an appropriate structure for the Web site and work to balance breadth and depth. Users go to a Web site looking for information to complete a task. Good design provides ease of navigation to allow users to find content quickly and easily.

During the design and development phase, you also should consider what, if any, types of multimedia could contribute positively to the Web site experience. For instance, adding a video message from the company CEO might be useful, but if the computing environment of your users cannot accommodate video playback, then the video serves no purpose. In general, do not use advanced multimedia technologies in a Web site, unless they make a positive contribution to the Web site experience.

Finally, consider accessibility issues and internationalization. A Web developer should always design for viewing by a diverse audience, including physically impaired and global users. A key consideration is that the software used by physically impaired individuals does not work with some Web features. For instance, if you use graphics on the Web site, always include alternate text for each graphic. To support an international audience, use generic icons that can be understood globally, avoid slang expressions in the content, and build simple pages that load quickly over lower-speed connections.

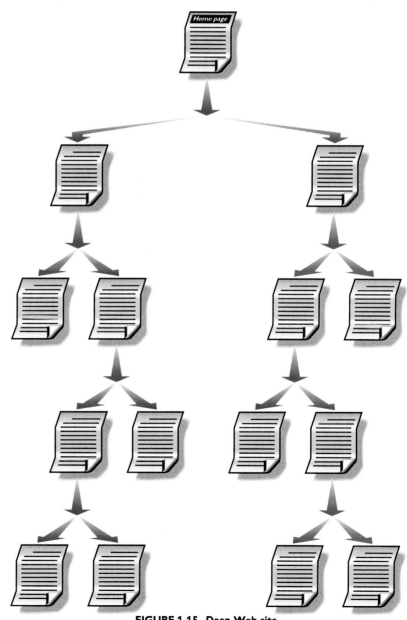

FIGURE 1-15 Deep Web site.

The design issues just discussed above are only a few of the basic Web page design issues that you need to consider. Throughout this book, design issues will be addressed as they relate to each project. Many excellent Web page design resources also are available on the Internet.

Web Site Testing

A Web site should be tested at various stages of the Web design and development processes. The testing process should be comprehensive and include a review of Web page content, functionality, and usability. Some basic steps to test content and functionality include:

- Proofreading content and page titles to review for accurate spelling and grammar
- Checking links to ensure they are not broken and are linked correctly
- Checking graphics to confirm they display properly and are linked correctly
- Ensuring that accessibility and internationalization issues are addressed
- Testing forms and other interactive page elements
- Testing pages to make sure they load quickly over lower-speed connections
- Printing each page to check how pages print
- Reviewing the HTML to ensure it meets W3C standards

You also should test each Web page in several different browser types and versions. Different browsers display some aspects of Web pages differently, so it is important to test Web pages in several different browsers to verify they display correctly in each browser. If you have used technologies that are not supported by older browsers or that require plug-ins, consider changing the content or providing alternate Web pages for viewing in older browsers.

Usability is the measure of how well a product, such as a Web site, allows a user to accomplish his or her goals. **Usability testing** is a method by which users of a Web site or other product are asked to perform certain tasks in an effort to measure the product's ease-of-use and the user's perception of the experience. Usability testing for a Web site should focus on three key aspects: content, navigation, and presentation.

Usability testing can be conducted in several ways. One good way to test a Web site's usability is to observe users interfacing with (or using) the Web site. As you observe users, you can track the links they click and record their actions and comments. You even can ask the users to explain what tasks they were trying to accomplish while navigating through the site. The information gained by observing users can be invaluable in helping to identify potential problem areas in the Web site. For example, if you observe that users have difficulty finding the Web page that lists store locations and hours of operation, you may want to clarify the link descriptions or make the links more prominent on the Web page.

Another way to conduct usability testing is to give users a specific task to complete (such as finding the product price list) and then observe how they navigate through the site to complete the task. If possible, ask them to explain why they selected certain links. Both of these observation methods are extremely valuable, but require access to users in order to conduct this type of testing.

Usability testing also can be completed using a questionnaire or survey. When writing a questionnaire or survey, be sure to write open-ended questions that can give you valuable information. For instance, asking the yes/no question, "Is the Web site visually appealing?," will not gather useful information. If you change that question to use a scaled response, such as, "Rate the visual appeal of this Web site, using a scale of 1 for low and 5 for high," you can get more valuable input from the users.

A usability testing questionnaire always should include space for users to write additional explanatory comments. For example, if a user rates the Web site's visual appeal as low and then adds a comment, you might learn that the user viewed the

Q: What other types of testing should be considered, in addition to usability testing?

A: For a newly implemented or maintained Web site, several types of tests should be conducted. Functionality testing involves determining if the Web site functions as it is designed to do. Compatibility testing is done to verify that the Web site works with a variety of browser versions. Stress testing determines what happens on your Web site when greater numbers of users access the site.

Q: What browsers should I use to test Web pages?

A: Use the browsers your audience is most likely to use. If your audience uses both PC and Macintosh computers, consider testing the Web pages using browsers on both platforms. You also may want to test the Web pages in several versions of the same browser (usually the two most recent versions), in the event users have not yet upgraded.

Web site on a smaller monitor that cut off the right side of the page, or you might find that the user disliked the site's background color.

Figure 1-16 shows some examples of types of questions and organization that you might include in a Web site usability testing questionnaire.

FIGURE 1-16 Web site usability testing questionnaire.

Web Site Implementation and Maintenance

Once Web site testing is complete and any required changes have been made, the Web site can be implemented. Implementation of a Web site involves the actual publishing of the Web pages to a Web server. Many HTML editors and WYSIWYG editors provide publishing capabilities. You also can use FTP software, such as WS_FTP, to publish your Web pages to a Web server. After you publish a Web site, you should test the Web pages again to confirm no obvious errors exist, such as broken links or missing graphics.

Once a site is implemented, develop a process to maintain the Web site. The one constant about Web development is that users will request changes and content will require updates. You need to ensure, however, that updates to the Web site do not compromise the site's integrity and consistency. For example, if you have a number of different people updating various Web pages on a large Web site, you might find it difficult to maintain a consistent look on pages across the Web site.

Q: How often should I update my Web site?

A: Plan to update your Web site on a regular basis to keep content up-to-date after your Web site is up and running. Do not allow your content to become stale, outdated, or include links to Web pages that no longer exist.

To help manage the task of Web site maintenance, first determine who is responsible for updates to content, structure, functionality, and so on. Then, limit the capability to update the Web site to specific users. Be sure the implementation is controlled by one or more Web developers who can verify that pages are tested thoroughly before the pages are published.

As updates and changes are made to a Web site, consider notifying users with a graphic banner or a "What's New" announcement, explaining any new features and how the features will benefit them. This technique not only keeps users informed, but also encourages them to come back to the Web site to see what is new.

Finally, Web site monitoring is another key aspect of maintaining a Web site. Usually, the Web servers that host Web sites keep logs of information about Web site usage. A **log** is the file that lists all of the Web pages that have been requested from the Web site. Web site logs are an invaluable source of information for a Web developer. Obtaining and analyzing the logs allows you to determine such things as: the number of visitors, browser types and versions, connection speeds, pages most commonly requested, and usage patterns. With this information, you can design a Web site that is effective for your targeted audience, providing them with a rich and rewarding experience.

> *More About*
>
> ## Log Files
>
> Usage statistics can provide a wealth of information about who is visiting your Web site and how they navigate through the Web site. To learn more about how log files work and how to analyze the information in those logs, visit the HTML More About Web page (scsite.com/html3e/more) and then click Log Files.

Project Summary

Project 1 provided an overview of the Internet and the World Wide Web and the key terms associated with those technologies. You then were introduced to the features and purposes of three different types of Web sites (the Internet, intranets, and extranets) and Web browsers used to view these sites. You also were presented with information about HTML, its history, elements, and coding standards, and its relationship to DHTML and XHTML. After reviewing various tools used to create HTML documents, you were provided an overview of the five phases of the Web development life cycle, along with pertinent questions to be addressed at each phase. It is important that a Web development project follow the life cycle methodology so the finished Web site is effective and efficient for the users. As you read the projects that follow in this book, you will gain an understanding of the power of HTML, as you learn how to develop many interesting and useful Web pages.

What You Should Know

Having completed this project, you should be able to perform the tasks below.

1. Describe the Internet (HTM 4)
2. Describe the World Wide Web (HTM 6)
3. Define Web servers (HTM 6)
4. Describe the Internet, intranets, and extranets (HTM 7)
5. Discuss Web browsers (HTM 9)
6. Define Hypertext Markup Language (HTM 9)
7. Outline the history of HTML (HTM 11)
8. Describe HTML elements (HTM 12)
9. List HTML coding practices (HTM 12)
10. Explain HTML versions (HTM 12)
11. Define Dynamic Hypertext Markup Language (HTM 13)
12. Define Extensible Hypertext Markup Language (HTM 13)
13. Describe tools for creating HTML documents (HTM 14)
14. Discuss the Web development life cycle (HTM 15)
15. Describe steps in the Web development planning phase (HTM 15)
16. Explain the Web development analysis phase (HTM 16)
17. Discuss Web design and development (HTM 17)
18. Describe various Web site structures (HTM 17)
19. Discuss the importance of Web site testing, including usability testing (HTM 20)
20. Discuss Web site implementation and maintenance (HTM 21)

Learn It Online

Instructions: To complete the Learn It Online exercises, start your browser, click the Address bar, and then enter the Web address scsite.com/html3e/learn. When the HTML Learn It Online page is displayed, follow the instructions in the exercises below. Each exercise has instructions for printing your results, either for your own records or for submission to your instructor.

1 Project Reinforcement TF, MC, and SA

Below HTML Project 1, click the Project Reinforcement link. Print the quiz by clicking Print on the File menu for each page. Answer each question.

2 Flash Cards

Below HTML Project 1, click the Flash Cards link and read the instructions. Type 20 (or a number specified by your instructor) in the Number of playing cards text box, type your name in the Enter your Name text box, and then click the Flip Card button. When the flash card is displayed, read the question and then click the ANSWER box arrow to select an answer. Flip through Flash Cards. If your score is 15 (75%) correct or greater, click Print on the File menu to print your results. If your score is less than 15 (75%) correct, then redo this exercise by clicking the Replay button.

3 Practice Test

Below HTML Project 1, click the Practice Test link. Answer each question, enter your first and last name at the bottom of the page, and then click the Grade Test button. When the graded practice test is displayed on your screen, click Print on the File menu to print a hard copy. Continue to take practice tests until you score 80% or better.

4 Who Wants To Be a Computer Genius?

Below HTML Project 1, click the Computer Genius link. Read the instructions, enter your first and last name at the bottom of the page, and then click the PLAY button. When your score is displayed, click the PRINT RESULTS link to print a hard copy.

5 Wheel of Terms

Below HTML Project 1, click the Wheel of Terms link. Read the instructions, and then enter your first and last name and your school name. Click the PLAY button. When your score is displayed, right-click the score and then click Print on the shortcut menu to print a hard copy.

6 Crossword Puzzle Challenge

Below HTML Project 1, click the Crossword Puzzle Challenge link. Read the instructions, and then enter your first and last name. Click the SUBMIT button. Work the crossword puzzle. When you are finished, click the Submit button. When the crossword puzzle is redisplayed, click the Print Puzzle button to print a hard copy.

7 Tips and Tricks

Below HTML Project 1, click the Tips and Tricks link. Click a topic that pertains to Project 1. Right-click the information and then click Print on the shortcut menu. Construct a brief example of what the information relates to in HTML to confirm you understand how to use the tip or trick.

8 Newsgroups

Below HTML Project 1, click the Newsgroups link. Click a topic that pertains to Project 1. Print three comments.

9 Expanding Your Horizons

Below HTML Project 1, click the Expanding Your Horizons link. Click a topic that pertains to Project 1. Print the information. Construct a brief example of what the information relates to in HTML to confirm you understand the contents of the article.

10 Search Sleuth

Below HTML Project 1, click the Search Sleuth link. To search for a term that pertains to this project, select a term below the Project 1 title and then use the Google search engine at google.com (or any major search engine) to display and print two Web pages that present information on the term.

11 Online Help I

Below HTML Project 1, click the Online Help I link. Follow the instructions on the page to access Web pages that provide additional help on project topics. Hand in any printed information to your instructor.

12 Online Help II

Below HTML Project 1, click the Online Help II link. Follow the instructions on the page to access Web pages that provide additional help on project topics. Hand in any printed information to your instructor.

1 Web Page Organizational Standards

Instructions: Start your word processing program. Open the file, apply1-1.doc, from the Project01\AYK folder on the HTML Data Disk. See the inside back cover of this book for instructions for downloading the Data Disk or see your instructor for information on accessing the files required for this book. As shown in Table 1-6, the apply1-1.doc file lists Web page organizational standards and the related reasons, but contains blanks in the Element column.

Table 1-6 Web Page Organizational Standards

ELEMENT	ORGANIZATIONAL STANDARD	REASON
	Use to explain purpose of page clearly	Helps user understand purpose of the page; identifies the page in search engine results
	Use to separate main topics	Makes a Web page easier to read; clearly explains what the page is about
	Use as a graphical element to separate main topics	Provides a graphic to break up Web page content
	Use to help divide large amounts of text	Provides shorter, more-readable sections of text
	Utilize these elements to organize text, when appropriate	Provides organized, easy-to-read text that readers can scan easily
	Use suitable amounts of information on each Web page	Increases likelihood that users view key information on a page, without needing to scroll

Perform the following tasks:

1. Without referring to Table 1-5 (on page HTM 17), determine the correct element that is described in the Organizational Standard and Reason columns.
2. Add the correct elements in the Element column.
3. Save the document using the file name, apply1-1solution.doc.
4. Print the document. Write your name on the printout and hand it in to your instructor.

1 Web Site Redesign

Problem: Figure 1-17 shows the popular online bookstore, Amazon.com. As you learned in this project, three common Web site structures include linear, hierarchical, and webbed. Based on that information, determine the structure used in the Amazon.com Web site. Review other similar Web sites and determine which Web site design features are beneficial to a user. Incorporate those ideas into a new Web site design for Amazon.com. Use paper to sketch out the new Web site design for the Amazon.com Web site.

FIGURE 1-17

Instructions: Perform the following steps using your browser and paper.

1. Start your browser. Open the Amazon.com Web site in your browser. Print the home page by clicking Print on the File menu.
2. Navigate through the Amazon.com Web site and determine the structure that the Web site utilizes (linear, hierarchical, or webbed) and write that on the printout.
3. Find two other online bookstore Web sites. Print the home pages for each of those sites by clicking Print on the File menu. Navigate through these Web sites to identify any Web site design features that are beneficial to a user.
4. Using ideas from the online bookstore Web sites that you found in Step 3, sketch a new Web site structure and design for the Amazon.com site on paper.
5. Write your name on the printouts and the sketch and hand them in to your instructor.

2 Student Club Web Site Design

Problem: You have decided to design a Web site that you can share with your student club members. In order to do this, you must complete the planning and analysis phases by answering such questions as:

*   What tasks will the student club members want to complete on the Web site?
*   What types of information should be included?
*   Who will provide information on the Web site content?

Interview several members of the student club and determine the answers to these questions. Based on that information, you will draw a sketch of a design for the home page of the student club Web site, such as the design shown in Figure 1-18.

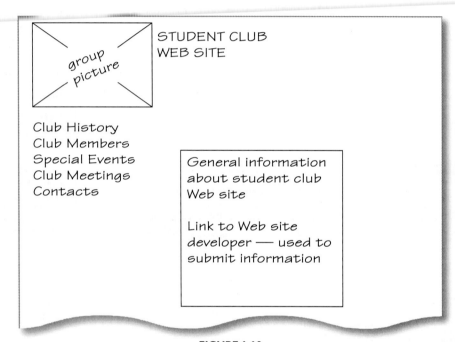

FIGURE 1-18

Instructions: Perform the following tasks using your word processing program and paper.

1. Review the questions in the planning and analysis phases of the Web development life cycle, as shown in Table 1-4 (on page HTM 16).
2. Assess the value of those questions listed in the table. Add other questions that you think are relevant to the planning and analysis of a student club Web site.
3. Start your word processing program. If necessary, open a new document. Enter the questions you will use for planning and analysis. Save the document using the file name, lab1-2solution.doc. Print the document.
4. Using the questions that you developed, interview student club members to determine what information should be included in the Web site, who will provide the information, and so on.
5. After gathering the required information, sketch a design for the home page of the Web site on paper.
6. Share your design sketch with members of the student club and get their opinions on your design.
7. Redraw the design on paper, making any changes based on the input from the club members.
8. Write Original Design on the first design sketch.
9. Write Second Design on the second design sketch.
10. Write your name on the printout and sketches and hand them in to your instructor.

3 Internet, Intranet, and Extranet Design

Problem: Three different types of Web sites were discussed in this project — Internet, intranet, and extranet. Each type of Web site type is designed for a different target audience. Think of a business (e.g., music, university, or bookstore) you frequently visit and how that business might use an Internet, intranet, and extranet site. Using the Planning phase questions found in Table 1-4 on page HTM 16, determine the answers to the questions listed in Table 1-7. Enter your ideas in the table. If there are questions that are difficult/impossible to answer directly (e.g., What are their computing environments?), list ways that you can use to find the answers to those questions.

Table 1-7 Planning Phase Questions			
TYPE OF BUSINESS			
PLANNING QUESTION	**INTERNET**	**INTRANET**	**EXTRANET**
What is the purpose of this Web site?			
Who will use this Web site?			
What are users' computing environments?			
Who owns and authors the information on the Web site?			
Who decides if/where the information goes on the Web site?			

Instructions: Perform the following tasks using your word processing program.

1. Start your word processing program and then open the file, lab1-3.doc, from the Project01\IntheLab folder on the HTML Data Disk.
2. Enter the type of business in the first row. Determine the answers to the first question for all three types of Web sites and then enter the answers in the appropriate table cells.
3. Continue answering the other four questions.
4. Save the file using the file name, lab1-3solution.doc. Print the document.
5. Write your name on the printout and hand it in to your instructor.

Cases and Places

The difficulty of these case studies varies: ▪ are the least difficult and ▪▪ are the most difficult. The last exercise is a group exercise.

1 ▪ A local job placement office wants to offer several of your company's online courses to their employees. A requirement of the job placement contract, however, is that the online courses must be accessible to users with disabilities and be Bobby Approved. Your manager has asked you to learn more about accessibility guidelines to determine what changes are needed to get the current online courses Bobby Approved. Visit the Bobby Web site at the URL, http://bobby.watchfire.com/bobby/html/en/index.jsp. Read the Web page to learn more about the Bobby tool. What types of disabilities do you have to consider when developing Web pages? What recommendations does Bobby make for accessibility? What does this mean for the Web page developer? View the information about getting your Web site Bobby Approved and read about the issues that are discussed there.

2 ▪ As a Web developer at D2 Design, you often are asked to restructure a client's existing Web sites to make them more user-friendly and easier to navigate. Find a Web site that utilizes more than one Web site structure (linear, hierarchical, and/or webbed). Is the information conveyed on the Web site displayed in the appropriate structure? Does the structure effectively support the information communicated? Print the home page of the Web site that you found. On a blank sheet of paper, sketch a design that you think might be more appropriate for the message. Use a word processing program to create a document that explains why your new design is more effective.

3 ▪▪ Johnson Smythe Interiors sells high-end furniture and carpets, along with its interior design services. The owner has hired you to give its Web site a new design that better captures the company's brand. Before starting on the design, you decide to create a list of Web design principles to which the Web site will adhere. Search the Web for more information about Web site design. Find three Web sites that give information about Web design principles. In a word processing document, take the ideas presented in this project together with the ideas presented in the other Web sites and make a comprehensive list of Web design principles. Where appropriate, identify any conflicting design principles discussed in the Web sites.

4 ▪▪ As the CarFoundry Webmaster, you are hoping to update your Web site to XHTML, but first want to learn more about how XHTML differs from HTML. Visit the W3Schools Web site (w3schools.com) to learn more about HTML and XHTML. In a word processing document, briefly describe HTML and XHTML, how they are related, and how they differ.

5 ▪▪ **Working Together:** Your manager at Travel Tours has asked your team to develop a usability survey or questionnaire that you can give to a group of users to evaluate the new online travel booking Web site. What types of information do you hope to gain by distributing this survey or questionnaire? How can you convey information on the survey or questionnaire so it clearly identifies what you are asking? Create a usability survey using your word processing program. Give the survey or questionnaire to at least five people. Allow them to complete the survey or questionnaire and then look at the results. If possible, ask the users what they thought the various questions conveyed. Is that what you wanted to convey? If not, think of other ways to gather the information that you need in a format that is self-explanatory.

HTML

Creating and Editing a Web Page

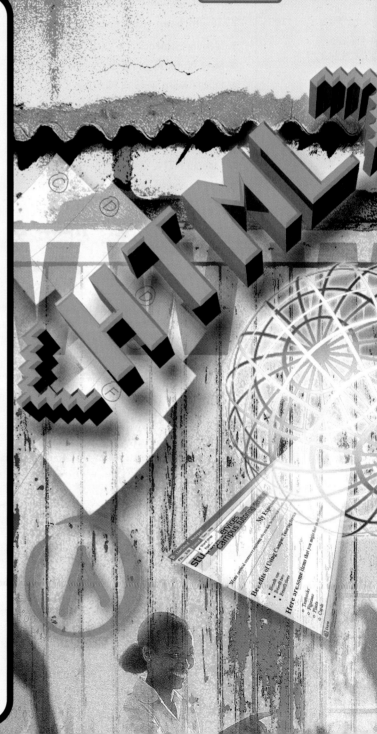

CASE PERSPECTIVE

Dr. Isabel Myers, the Dean of Student Services, is very concerned about the academic success of all students, especially freshman students. Recent statistics, however, show that many students do not pass several freshman-level classes their first time taken. Dr. Myers has an idea to use student workers, who previously have passed these courses with a grade of A, as tutors for struggling students. She thinks students who recently completed the courses successfully will have an easier time relating to the questions asked by the students who need some help. Dr. Myers knows something about the World Wide Web (also called the Web) and wonders if the Campus Tutoring Service should develop its own Web site to advertise the new service. She came to you, an MIS major, to ask for your help.

After working with Dr. Myers to plan the Web site and analyze required Web site content and functionality, you start to design and develop a Web page that promotes the Campus Tutoring Service's key services (Figure 2-1a on page HTM 31). To develop this Web page, you will use Hypertext Markup Language (HTML), as shown in Figure 2-1b. You begin the project with a simple text Web page. You then will visually enhance the Web pages by using various text sizes and formats, adding color, and including an image and a horizontal rule. You also will add a bulleted list to organize the information on the Web page. Once finished with the development, you will review the Web page with Dr. Myers for modifications, enhancements, or additional Web page developments.

As you read through this project, you will learn how to use Notepad to create a Web page using HTML, enhance the look of a Web page, and save and print an HTML file.

Creating and Editing a Web Page

Objectives

You will have mastered the material in this project when you can:

- Identify elements of a Web page
- Start Notepad and describe the Notepad window
- Enable word wrap in Notepad
- Enter the HTML tags
- Enter headings and a paragraph of text
- Create an unordered, ordered, or definition list
- Save an HTML file
- Use a browser to view a Web page
- Activate Notepad
- Identify Web page image types and attributes
- Add an image, change the background color of a Web page, center a heading, and add a horizontal rule
- View the HTML source code in a browser
- Print a Web page and an HTML file
- Quit Notepad and a browser

Introduction

With an understanding of the Web development life cycle, you should have a good idea about the importance of proper Web site planning, analysis, and design. After completing these phases, the next phase is the actual development of a Web page using HTML. As discussed in Project 1, Web pages are created using HTML, which uses a set of special tags to define the structure, layout, and appearance of a Web page. In this project, you will learn to create a Web page by entering HTML into the Notepad window and then saving the file as an HTML file. After entering basic HTML tags and adding text to the file, you will learn the tags used to organize the text by adding headings and creating a bulleted list. You then will learn how to enhance the Web page's appearance by inserting an image, changing the background color of the Web page, centering a heading, and adding a horizontal rule. Finally, you will learn to view the Web page and HTML code in your browser and then print the Web page from your browser.

Project Two — The Campus Tutoring Service

Project 2 illustrates how to use HTML to create a Web page for the Campus Tutoring Service, as shown in Figure 2-1a. Before building the first Web page, you must plan the purpose of the Web page and then analyze what content to include. The Campus Tutoring Service Web page will include general information about the new tutoring service, along with contact information and the list of courses for which tutors are available. To make the Web page interesting, you will use various HTML tags to format the paragraphs and add a bulleted list. You also will insert a colorful image, add a horizontal rule, and change the background color to make the Web page more appealing.

To edit text and HTML tags used to create the Web page, you use a program called Notepad, as shown in Figure 2-1b. **Notepad** is a basic text editor you can use for simple documents or for creating Web pages using HTML. You also will use the Microsoft Internet Explorer browser to view your Web page as you create it. By default, Notepad and Internet Explorer are installed with Windows, so these two programs should be available on most computers running Windows. If you do not have Notepad or Internet Explorer available on your computer, other text editor or browser programs will work.

Q&A

Q: I plan to use a WYSIWYG editor to create Web pages. Why should I learn HTML?

A: Understanding HTML is an important aspect of being a well-rounded Web developer. Although popular WYSIWYG editors, such as Microsoft FrontPage and Macromedia Dreamweaver, automatically create HTML code as you add elements to the Web page, you still should understand the resulting HTML code. Understanding HTML will allow you to edit the HTML code directly to make modifications not supported by the WYSIWYG editor.

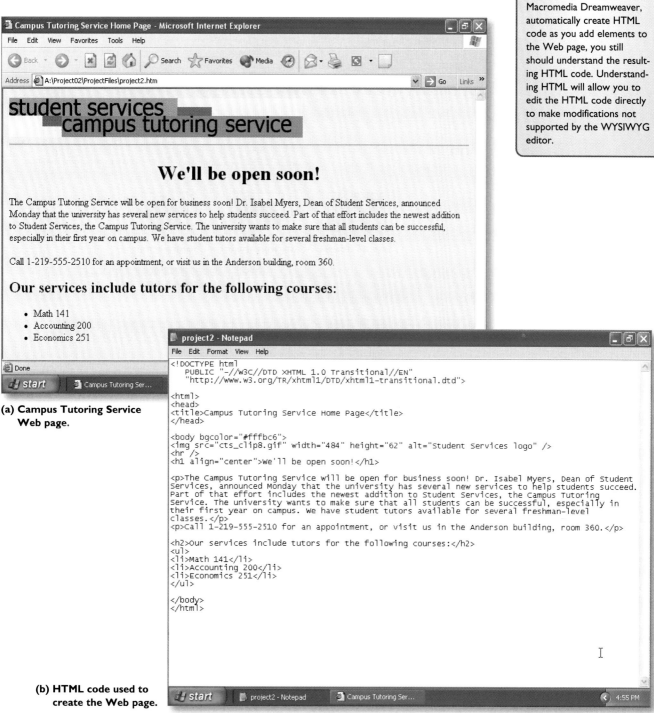

(a) Campus Tutoring Service Web page.

(b) HTML code used to create the Web page.

FIGURE 2-1

Elements of a Web Page

Today, many people — individuals, students, teachers, business executives, Web developers, and others — are developing Web pages for personal or professional reasons. Each person has his or her own style and the resulting Web pages are as diverse as the people who create them. Most Web pages, however, include several basic features, or elements, as shown in Figure 2-2.

FIGURE 2-2 Elements of a Web page.

Window Elements

The **title** of a Web page is the text that appears on the title bar of the browser window when the Web page appears. The title also is the name assigned to the page if a user adds the page to the browser's list of **favorites**, or **bookmarks**. Because of its importance, you always should include a title on your Web page. The title, which usually is the first element you see, should identify the subject or purpose of the page. The title should be concise yet descriptive and briefly explain the page's content or purpose to the visitor.

The **body** of the Web page contains the information that is displayed in the browser window. The body can include text, graphics, and other elements. The **background** of a Web page is a solid color or a picture or graphic against which the other elements on the Web page appear. When choosing your background, be sure it does not overpower the information on the Web page. If you use an image for the background, the image is tiled, or repeats across and down the page, similar to the Wallpaper in Windows.

Text Elements

Normal text is the default text format used for the main content of a Web page. Normal text can be used in a standard paragraph or formatted to appear as bold (<strong>), italic (<em>), or underlined text (<u>); in different colors; and so on.

Normal text also can be used in a series of text items called a **list**. Typically, lists are bulleted or numbered.

Headings, such as those in Figure 2-2, are used to set off different paragraphs of text or different sections of a page. Headings are a larger font size than normal text and often are bold or italic or a different color than normal text. HTML has six different sizes, or levels, of headings numbered 1 through 6, with 1 being the largest. When using headings to organize content and emphasize key points on a Web page, be sure to use headings consistently. That is, if you use a Heading 2 (<h2>) style for a specific level of text, you always should use a Heading 2 style to break up information at that level. Also, do not skip levels of headings in your document. For example, do not start with a Heading 1 (<h1>) style and then use a Heading 3 (<h3>) style.

Image Elements

Web pages typically use several different types of graphics, or images, such as an icon, bullet, line, photo, illustration, or other picture. An image used in a Web page also is called an **inline image**, which means the image or graphic file is not part of the HTML file. Instead, the Web browser merges the separate graphic file into the Web page as it is displayed in the browser window. The HTML file contains <img> tags that tell the browser which graphic file to request from the server, where to insert it on the page, and how to display it.

Web pages typically use several different types of inline images. An **image map** is a special type of inline image in which you define one or more areas as hotspots. A **hotspot** is an area of an image that activates a function when selected. For example, each hotspot in an image map can link to a different Web page. Some inline images are **animated**, meaning they include motion and can change in appearance.

Horizontal rules are lines that are displayed across a Web page to separate different sections of the page. Although the appearance of a horizontal rule can vary, many Web pages use an inline image as a horizontal rule. Alternatively, you can use the horizontal rule tag (<hr />) to add a simple horizontal rule, such as the one used in this project.

When including images on a Web page, be cautious about overuse. Using too many images may give your Web page a cluttered look or distract the visitor from the purpose of the Web page. An image should have a purpose, such as to convey content, visually organize a page, provide a hyperlink, or serve another function.

Hyperlink Elements

One of the more important elements of a Web page is a hyperlink, or link. A **link** is text, an image, or another Web page element that you click to instruct the browser to go to a location in a file or to request a file from a server. On the Web, links are the primary way to navigate between Web pages and among Web sites. Links point not only to Web pages, but also to graphics, sound, video, program files, e-mail addresses, and parts of the same Web page. Text links, also called hypertext links, are the most commonly used hyperlinks. When text identifies a hyperlink, it usually appears as underlined text, in a color different from the rest of the Web page text.

Starting Notepad

With the planning, analysis, and design of the Web page complete, you can begin developing the Web page by entering HTML in the Notepad window. The steps on the next page show how to start Notepad.

More About

HTML

The Web has many wonderful sources of information on HTML and Web page development. One of the better sources is the HTML Goodies Web site, which has primers and tutorials on a variety of topics as well as free downloads and discussion areas. To learn more about this Web site, visit the HTML More About Web page (scsite.com/html3e/more) and then click HTML Goodies.

To Start Notepad

1

• **Click the Start button on the Windows taskbar.**

• **Click All Programs on the Start menu.**

• **Point to Accessories on the All Programs submenu and then point to Notepad on the Accessories submenu (Figure 2-3).**

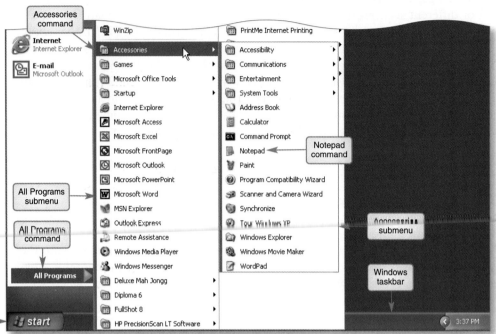

FIGURE 2-3

2

• **Click Notepad.**

The Notepad window is displayed (Figure 2-4).

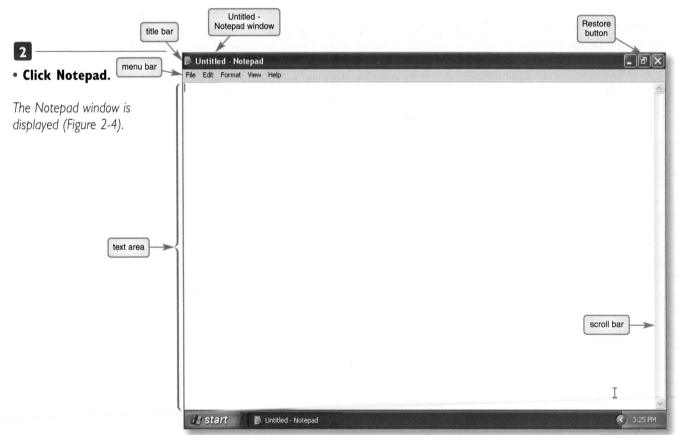

FIGURE 2-4

If the Notepad window is not maximized, click the Maximize button on the Notepad title bar to maximize it.

The Notepad Window

The Notepad window contains several elements similar to document windows in other applications. The main elements of the Notepad window are the title bar, the menu bar, the text area, and the scroll bars (Figure 2-4).

Title Bar

The **title bar** appears at the top of the Notepad window. The name of the document open in the Notepad window is displayed. When you first start Notepad, the default document is named Untitled.

Menu Bar

The **menu bar** appears at the top of the window just below the title bar (Figure 2-4). The menu bar shows Notepad menu names. Each **menu name** represents a menu. A **menu** provides a list of commands you can use to open, save, and print the text in the file and perform other tasks.

Text Area

The **text area** is the main part of the Notepad window (Figure 2-4). As you type, text is displayed in the text area.

Scroll Bar

On the right side of the Notepad window is a vertical **scroll bar**, which is used to view different portions of the text area (Figure 2-4). The **scroll box** on the scroll bar indicates your current location in the file. If all of the text in the file appears in the Notepad window, as shown in Figure 2-4, the scroll bar is dimmed and the scroll box does not display.

More About

WordPad

WordPad is another text editor that you can use to create HTML files. To start WordPad, click the Start button on the taskbar, point to All Programs on the Start menu, point to Accessories on the All Programs submenu, and then click WordPad on the Accessories submenu. WordPad help provides tips on how to use the product.

Enabling Word Wrap in Notepad

In Notepad, the text entered in the text area scrolls continuously to the right unless the Word Wrap feature is enabled, or turned on. **Word wrap** causes text lines to break at the right edge of the window and appear on a new line, so all entered text is visible in the Notepad window. Word wrap does not affect the way text prints. When word wrap is enabled, a check mark precedes the Word Wrap command on the Format menu. The steps on the next page show how to enable word wrap in Notepad.

To Enable Word Wrap in Notepad

1

• Click **Format** on the menu bar (Figure 2-5).

2

• If the **Word Wrap** command does not have a check mark next to it, click **Word Wrap**.

Notepad enables word wrap so the text will not scroll off the screen as you type.

FIGURE 2-5

Entering HTML Tags and Text

To create an HTML document, you begin by inserting a <!DOCTYPE> tag and four sets of tags (<html>, <head>, <title>, and <body>). These tags define the overall structure of a standard Web page and divide the HTML file into its basic sections, such as the header information and the body of the page that contains text and graphics.

Entering HTML Tags to Define the Web Page Structure

The **<!DOCTYPE>** tag is used to tell the browser which HTML or XHTML version and type the document uses. The W3C supports three document types for HTML or XHTML: *strict*, *transitional*, and *frameset*. The **strict** document type is specified when you want to prohibit the use of deprecated tags. **Deprecated tags** are tags that the W3C has earmarked for eventual removal from their specifications, because they have replaced those tags with newer, more functional tags. The **transitional** document type allows the use of deprecated tags. The **frameset** document type, which is used to support frames on a Web page, also allows the use of deprecated tags. The <!DOCTYPE> tag includes a URL that references a Document Type Definition found on the W3C Web site. A **Document Type Definition (DTD)** is a file containing definitions of tags and how they should be used in a Web page. Projects 2 through 5 use a transitional document type. Projects 6 and 7 use a frameset document type, because those projects utilize frames.

The second set of tags, **<html>** and **</html>**, indicates the start and end of an HTML document. Software tools, such as browsers, use these tags to determine where the HTML code in a file begins and ends. The third set of tags, **<head>** and **</head>**, contains the Web page title and other document header information. The fourth set of tags, **<title>** and **</title>**, indicates the title of the Web page. As previously noted, the title appears on the browser title bar when the Web page is displayed in the browser window. The title also is the name that appears in the favorite or bookmark when a user adds the page to the favorite or bookmark list. The final set of tags, **<body>** and **</body>**, indicates the boundaries of the Web page. All text, images, links, and other content is contained within this final set of tags.

To make your HTML files compliant with XHTML standards, always enter tags in lowercase (with the exception of the <!DOCTYPE> tag, which is always uppercase). Throughout this book, the project directions follow these standards to help you learn good HTML and XHTML coding standards.

Most HTML start tags, such as <html>, <head>, <title>, and <body>, also have corresponding end tags, </html>, </head>, </title>, and </body>. Table 2-1 lists the functions of those tags as well as other tags that you use in this project. Note that, for tags that do not have end tags, such as <hr /> and <br />, the tag is closed using a space and a forward slash.

Table 2-1 HTML Tags and Their Functions	
HTML TAG	**FUNCTION**
<!DOCTYPE>	Indicates the version and type of HTML used; includes a URL reference to a DTD
<html> </html>	Indicates the start and end of an HTML document
<head> </head>	Indicates the start and end of a section of the document used for the title and other document header information
<title> </title>	Indicates the start and end of the title. The title does not appear in the body of the Web page, but appears on the title bar of the browser.
<body> </body>	Indicates the start and end of the Web page body
<hn> </hn>	Indicates the start and end of the text section called a heading; sizes range from <h1> through <h6>. See Figure 2-8a on page HTM 39 for heading size samples.
<p> </p>	Indicates the start of a new paragraph; inserts a blank line above the new paragraph
<ul> </ul>	Indicates the start and end of an unordered (bulleted) list
<li> </li>	Indicates that the item that follows the tag is an item within a list
<hr />	Inserts a horizontal rule

	Inserts a line break at the point where the tag appears

The steps on the next page illustrate how to enter the initial tags that define the structure of the Web page.

More About

HTML and XHTML Tags

The Web has excellent sources that list HTML and XHTML tags. For more information about HTML and XHTML, visit the HTML More About Web page (scsite.com/html3e/more.htm) and then click HTML and XHTML.

More About

The DOCTYPE Tag

The W3Schools Web site provides additional information about the DOCTYPE tags used for the strict, transitional, and frameset document types. To learn more about the DOCTYPE tag, visit the HTML More About Web page (scsite.com/html3e/more.htm) and then click DOCTYPE tags.

To Enter HTML Tags to Define the Web Page Structure

1

• **Type** `<!DOCTYPE html` **and then press the ENTER key.**

• **Press the SPACEBAR three times, type** `PUBLIC "-//W3C//DTD XHTML 1.0 Transitional//EN"` **as the entry, and then press the ENTER key.**

• **Press the SPACEBAR three times, type** `"http://www.w3 .org/TR/xhtml1/DTD/xhtml1- transitional.dtd">` **as the entry, and then press the ENTER key twice.**

• **Type** `<html>` **and then press the ENTER key.**

• **Type** `<head>` **and then press the ENTER key.**

• **Type** `<title>Campus Tutoring Service Home Page</title>` **and then press the ENTER key.**

• **Type** `</head>` **and then press the ENTER key.**

The HTML tags are displayed in the Notepad window (Figure 2-6). The text between the title tags is displayed when you view the Web page using a browser. The </title> tag indicates the title is complete and the </head> tag indicates the headings are complete.

FIGURE 2-6

2

• **Type** `<body>` **and then press the ENTER key twice.**

• **Type** `</body>` **and then press the ENTER key.**

• **Type** `</html>` **as the end tag.**

The <body> tag starts the body section of the Web page and the </body> tag ends the body section. The </html> tag (Figure 2-7) ends the HTML file itself. The remainder of the HTML tags will be entered between the <body> and </body> tags.

FIGURE 2-7

If you notice an error in the text, use the BACKSPACE key to delete all the characters back to and including the incorrect characters and then continue typing.

Entering Headings

Headings serve to separate text and introduce new topics on Web pages. The headings used for this purpose vary in size. The tags used to specify the heading style or sizes range from <h1> through <h6>, with <h1> being the largest. Figure 2-8a shows a Web page using various sizes of headings. One method of maintaining a consistent look on a Web page is to use the same heading size for headings at the same topic level (Figure 2-8b).

The step on the next page explains how to enter the first heading for the Web page.

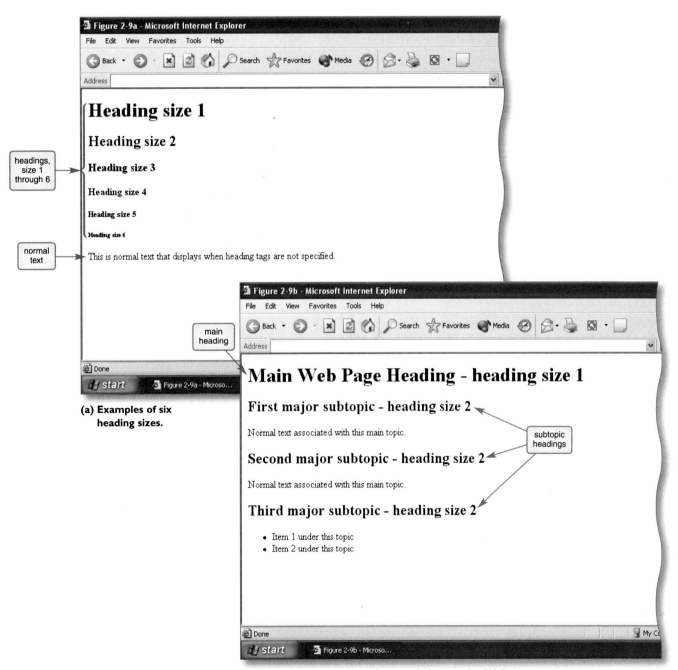

(a) Examples of six
heading sizes.

(b) A consistent use of headings can help organize Web page content.

FIGURE 2-8

To Enter a Heading

1

• **Click the blank line below the** **<body> tag, type** <h1>We'll be open soon!</h1> **in the text area, and then press the ENTER key twice.**

The HTML code is displayed (Figure 2-9). The main heading is formatted using the Heading 1 (<h1>) style. An additional space line was inserted for readability.

FIGURE 2-9

The <h1> tag is used to apply a Heading 1 style to the main heading on a Web page because it is the largest heading size. The main heading often presents the most important message on a Web page or contains the name of the business, school, or organization. A Web page usually has only one main heading; the HTML file for that Web page thus usually has only one set of <h1> </h1> tags.

Entering a Paragraph of Text

Web pages generally contain a significant amount of text. Breaking the text into paragraphs helps to separate key ideas and make the text easier to read. The <p> start tag is used to indicate the start of a new paragraph. When the browser finds a <p> tag in an HTML file, it starts a new line and inserts a blank line above the new paragraph. The </p> end tag indicates the end of the paragraph.

The following steps illustrate how to enter a paragraph of text in an HTML file.

To Enter a Paragraph of Text

1

• **With the insertion point on line 12, press the ENTER key and then type** <p>The Campus Tutoring Service will be open for business soon! Dr. Isabel Myers, Dean of Student Services, announced Monday that the university has several new services to help students succeed. Part of that effort includes the newest addition to Student Services, the Campus Tutoring Service. The university wants to make sure that all students can be successful, especially in their first year on campus. We have student tutors available for several freshman-level classes.</p> **and then press the ENTER key.**

2

• **With the insertion point on line 19, type** <p>Call 1-219-555-2510 for an appointment, or visit us in the Anderson building, room 360.</p> **and then press the ENTER key twice (Figure 2-10).**

line 19

start of paragraph

paragraph text

end of paragraph

FIGURE 2-10

The <br /> tag also is used to break a line of text. As soon as the browser encounters a <br /> tag, it starts a new line with the text that follows the tag. Unlike the <p> tag, using the <br /> tag does not insert a blank line above the new line of text. The <br /> tag is used later in this book.

Creating a List

Text on a Web page sometimes is easier for users to read and understand when it is formatted as a list, instead of as a paragraph format. Lists structure text into an itemized format. Typically, lists are bulleted (unordered) or numbered (ordered).

An **unordered list**, which also is called a **bulleted list,** formats information using small images called bullets. Figure 2-11 on the next page shows Web page text formatted as unordered, or bulleted, lists and the HTML code used to create the lists.

An **ordered list**, which also is called a **numbered list**, formats information in a series using numbers or letters. An ordered list works well to organize items where order must be emphasized, such as a series of steps. Figure 2-12 on the next page shows Web page text formatted as ordered, or numbered, lists and the HTML tags used to create the lists.

The **<ul>** and **</ul>** tags must be at the start and end of an unordered or bulleted list. The **<ol>** and **</ol>** tags are used at the start and end of an ordered or numbered list. Unordered and ordered lists have optional bullet and number types. As shown in Figure 2-11, an unordered list can use one of three different bullet options: disc, square, or circle. If no type is identified, the default, disc, is used. An ordered list can use numbers, letters, or Roman numerals, as shown in Figure 2-12. The default option is to use Arabic numbers, such as 1, 2, and 3.

The format of the start tag for a list without a bullet and number type specified is <ul> or <ol>. To change the default bullet or number type, the **type** attribute is entered within the <ol> or <ul> tags. The tags <ul type=" "> or <ol type=" "> create lists that use a specific bullet and number type, where the specified type is found within the quotation marks.

After the <ul> or <ol> tag is entered to define the type of list, the **<li>** and **</li>** tags are used to define a list item in an ordered or unordered list. As shown in Figures 2-11 and 2-12, each item in a list must have the <li> tag at the start and the </li> tag at the end.

FIGURE 2-11 Examples of unordered (bulleted) lists.

FIGURE 2-12 Examples of ordered (numbered) lists.

The following steps illustrate how to create an unordered, or bulleted, list using the default bullet style.

To Create an Unordered List

1

• **With the insertion point on line 20, press the ENTER key, type** <h2>Our services include tutors for the following courses:</h2> **as the entry, and then press the ENTER key.**

2

• **Type** <ul> **as the start tag and then press the ENTER key.**

• **Type** <li>Math 141</li> **and then press the ENTER key.**

• **Type** <li>Accounting 200</li> **and then press the ENTER key.**

• **Type** <li>Economics 251</li> **and then press the ENTER key.**

• **Type** </ul> **as the end tag and then press the ENTER key.**

The HTML code creates a bulleted list with three items (Figure 2-13). Because the code does not specify a type attribute, the list uses the default disc bullet.

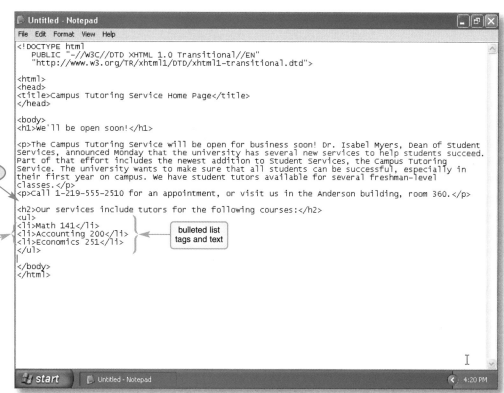

FIGURE 2-13

A third type of list, called a **definition list**, offsets information in a dictionary-like style. While used less often than unordered or ordered lists, definition lists are useful to create a glossary-like list of terms and definitions, as shown in Figure 2-14a on the next page. Figure 2-14b shows the HTML code used to create the definition list.

The syntax for definition lists is not as straightforward as the <ul>, <ol>, or <li> structure that is used in the unordered and ordered list styles. With definition lists, you use the **<dl>** and **</dl>** tags to start and end the list. A **<dt>** tag indicates a term and a **<dd>** tag identifies the definition of that term by offsetting the definition from the term. Table 2-2 on the next page lists the elements of a definition list and their purposes.

(a) Example of a definition list.

(b) HTML code used to create a definition list.

FIGURE 2-14

Table 2-2 Definition List Elements and Purposes	
DEFINITION LIST ELEMENT	PURPOSE
<dl> </dl>	Used to start and end a definition list
<dt>	Used to identify a term
<dd>	Used to identify the definition of the term directly above

The start <dl> tag indicates the start of a definition list. After the <dl> tag, the <dt> tag is used to identify a term, followed by the <dd> tag to provide the definition of that term. The end </dl> tag identifies the end of a definition list. As shown in Figures 2-14a and 2-14b, by default, the definition term is left-aligned on the line and the definition for each term is indented so it easily is distinguishable as the definition for the term above.

Saving an HTML File

After entering code in the HTML file, you should view the Web page in a browser to see what the Web page looks like up to this point. In general, viewing the Web page periodically during development is good coding practice, as it allows you to see the effect of various HTML tags on the text. To view the Web page in a browser, the HTML file first must be saved.

HTML files must end with an extension of **.htm** or **.html**. HTML files with an extension of .html can be viewed on Web servers running an operating system that allows long file names. Web servers with Windows Server 2003, Windows XP, Windows 2000, Windows NT, or Macintosh operating systems all allow long file names. For Web servers that run an operating system that does not accept long file names, you need the .htm extension. In this book, all files are saved using the .htm extension. The following steps show how to save an HTML file.

More About

HTML File Names

HTML files have an extension of .html or .htm. Generally, the home page of a Web site is called index.html or index.htm. Many service providers default to this name as the first page of a Web site to display.

To Save an HTML File

1

• **With a floppy disk in drive A, click File on the menu bar (Figure 2-15).**

FIGURE 2-15

2

• **Click Save As on the File menu.**

The Save As dialog box is displayed (Figure 2-16).

FIGURE 2-16

3

• **Type** project2.htm **in the File name text box.**

• **Click the Save in box arrow.**

The file name, project2.htm, appears in the File name text box (Figure 2-17). Notepad displays a list of available drives and folders.

FIGURE 2-17

4

• **Click 3½ Floppy (A:) in the Save in list.**

• **Click the Project02 folder and then double-click the ProjectFiles folder in the list of available folders.**

The Project02\ProjectFiles folder on Drive A becomes the selected drive (Figure 2-18).

FIGURE 2-18

title bar displays
new file name,
project2

5

• **Click the Save button in the Save As dialog box.**

Notepad saves the HTML file in the Project02\ProjectFiles folder on the floppy disk in drive A using the file name, project2.htm. Although the HTML file is saved on a floppy disk, it also remains in memory and is displayed on the screen (Figure 2-19). Notepad displays the new file name on the title bar.

project2 - Notepad

File Edit Format View Help

```
<!DOCTYPE html
    PUBLIC "-//W3C//DTD XHTML 1.0 Transitional//EN"
    "http://www.w3.org/TR/xhtml1/DTD/xhtml1-transitional.dtd">

<html>
<head>
<title>Campus Tutoring Service Home Page</title>
</head>

<body>
<h1>We'll be open soon!</h1>

<p>The Campus Tutoring Service will be open for business soon! Dr. Isabel Myers, Dean
Services, announced Monday that the university has several new services to help studen
Part of that effort includes the newest addition to Student Services, the Campus Tutori
Service. The university wants to make sure that all students can be successful, especia
their first year on campus. We have student tutors available for several freshman-level
classes.</p>
<p>Call 1-219-555-2510 for an appointment, or visit us in the Anderson building, room 3
```

FIGURE 2-19

Using a Browser to View a Web Page

After saving an HTML file, you can use a browser to view your Web page. The HTML file is displayed in the browser as if the file were available on the Web.

Starting a Browser

An important feature of Windows is its **multitasking** capability — that is, its capability to have more than one program or process running at the same time. With the HTML file saved on a floppy disk in drive A, the next step is to view the Web page using a browser. The following steps illustrate how to start a browser to view a Web page.

To Start a Browser

1

• **Click the Start button on the Windows taskbar and then point to All Programs on the Start menu (Figure 2-20).**

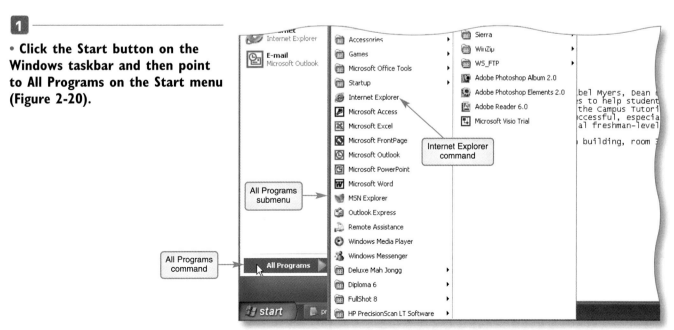

FIGURE 2-20

2

• **Click Internet Explorer (or another browser command) on the All Programs submenu. If necessary, click the Maximize button to maximize the browser window.**

The browser displays a Web page (Figure 2-21). The title of the Web page appears on the browser title bar. A different Web page may appear in your browser.

FIGURE 2-21

More About

User Interface Design

The user interface design is a very important aspect of a Web site. If a site is designed poorly, users may be unable to find the desired information or complete a task, which makes the Web site ineffective. To learn more about good Web design principles, visit the HTML More About Web page (scsite.com/html3e/more) and then click Web Design.

If your computer is connected to the Internet when the browser window opens, it displays a **home page**, or **start page**, which is a Web page that appears each time Internet Explorer starts. Because it is possible to customize browser settings to change the Web page that appears as the home page, the home page displayed by your browser may be different. Schools and organizations often set a main page on their Web sites as the home page for browsers installed on lab or office computers.

Viewing a Web Page in a Browser

A browser allows you to open a file located on your computer and have full browsing capabilities, as if the Web page were stored on a Web server and made available on the Web. The following steps use this technique to view the HTML file, project2.htm, in a browser.

To View a Web Page in a Browser

1

- **When the browser window appears, click the Address bar.**

- **Type** a:\Project02\ ProjectFiles\project2.htm **in the Address box.**

The URL is displayed in the Address box (Figure 2-22). If you type an incorrect letter or symbol in the Address box and notice the error before moving to the next step, use the BACKSPACE key to erase all the characters back to and including the one that is incorrect and then continue typing.

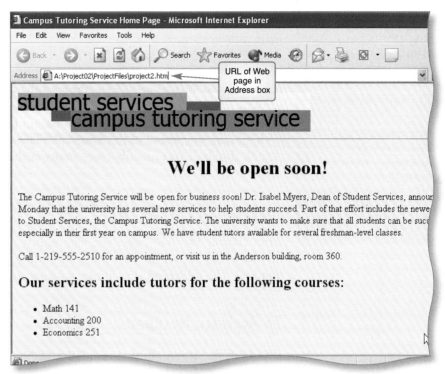

FIGURE 2-22

2

- **Press the ENTER key.**

The browser displays the Web page, project2.htm (Figure 2-23). The Address box appears with A:\Project02\ProjectFiles\ project2.htm, which indicates the HTML file is saved on the floppy disk in drive A.

FIGURE 2-23

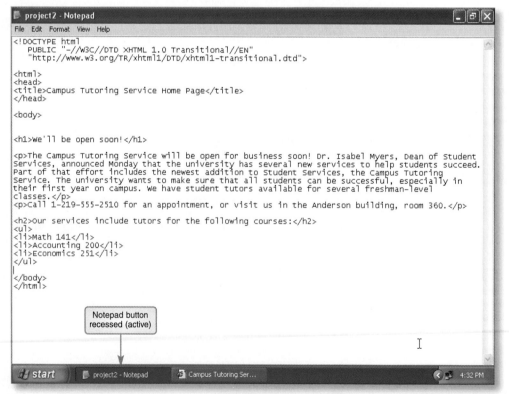 *More About*

Developing Web Pages for Multiple Browsers

When developing Web pages, you must consider the types of browsers visitors will use, including Internet Explorer and Netscape Navigator for Windows or Safari or Internet Explorer for MacOS. The Apple Web site provides suggestions for creating Web pages that will work in a wide range of browsers. Visit the HTML More About Web page (scsite.com/html3e/more) and then click Developing for Multiple Browsers.

The browser displays the Web page as if it were available on the Web. Viewing Web pages periodically during development ensures that the Web pages appear in the manner you intend. To understand the HTML code used to create the Web page, compare the Web page displayed in the browser with the HTML file in Notepad. The title bar, for example, displays the Campus Tutoring Service Home Page, which is the title text entered on line 7 of the HTML file. All the information contained in the body of the Web page — that is, between the <body> and </body> tags — now appears in the browser window. The main heading, We'll be open soon!, appears larger because it is tagged as Heading 1 (<h1>) style, whereas the heading, Our services include tutors for the following courses:, appears smaller because it is tagged as a Heading 2 (<h2>) style. The two paragraphs of text appear using normal font, with a blank line above each paragraph. The unordered (bulleted) list uses the default disc bullet to identify three items in the list.

Activating Notepad

After viewing the Web page, you can modify the Web page by adding additional tags or text to the HTML file. To continue editing, you first must return to the Notepad window. The following step illustrates how to activate Notepad.

To Activate Notepad

1 **Click the Notepad button on the taskbar.**

The maximized Notepad window becomes the active window (Figure 2-24).

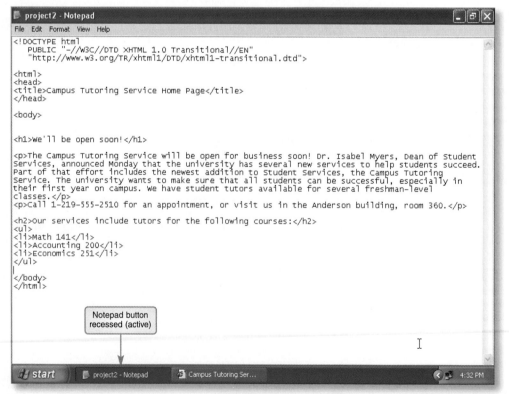

FIGURE 2-24

Web Page Images

Images are used in many ways to enhance the look of a Web page and make it more interesting and colorful. Images can be used to add background color, to help organize a Web page, to help clarify a point being made in the text, or to serve as links to other Web pages. Images also often are used to break up Web page sections (such as a horizontal rule) or as directional elements that allow a visitor to navigate through a Web site.

Image Types

Web pages use three types of files as images: GIF, JPEG, and PNG. **Graphics Interchange Format** (**GIF**) files have an extension of .gif. A graphic image saved as a GIF (pronounced *jiff* or *giff*) also is saved using compression techniques to make it smaller for download on the Web. The technique used to compress GIF files (called LZW compression) is patented, however, which means companies making products that use the GIF format must obtain a license. This does not apply to typical Web users or businesses that include GIFs in their Web pages. Standard (or non-interlaced) GIF images are displayed one line at a time when loading. Interlaced GIF images load all at once, starting with a blurry look and becoming sharper as they load. Using interlaced GIFs for large images is a good technique, because a Web page visitor can see a blurred outline of the image as it loads. Users with faster Internet connections most likely will see little difference between an interlaced GIF and a non-interlaced GIF.

Joint Photographic Experts Group (**JPEG**) files have an extension of .jpg, .jpe, or .jpeg. A JPEG (pronounced *JAY-peg*) is a graphic image saved using compression techniques to make it smaller for download on the Web. When creating a JPEG image, you can specify the image quality to reach a balance between image quality and file size. JPEG files often are used for more complex images, such as photographs, because the JPEG file format supports more colors and resolutions than the other file types.

A third type of image file is **Portable Network Graphics** (**PNG**), which has a .png or .ping extension. The PNG (pronounced *ping*) format also is a compressed file format that supports multiple colors and resolutions. The World Wide Web Consortium developed the PNG format as a graphics standard and patent-free alternative to the GIF format. Most newer browsers support PNG images.

If an image is not in one of these formats, you can use a paint or graphics-editing program to convert an image to a .gif, .jpg, or .png format. Some paint programs even allow you to save a GIF image as interlaced. A number of paint and graphics-editing programs, such Adobe Photoshop, Corel Painter, and Jasc Paint Shop Pro, are available in the marketplace today.

Image Attributes

Table 2-3 on the next page lists the attributes that can be used with the <img> tag. In this project, the src and alt attributes are used in the <img> tag. The **src** attribute is used to define the URL of the image to load. The **alt** attribute is used to provide alternative text, in the event the image is not displayed. The alt text is especially useful to vision-impaired users who use a screen reader, which translates information on a computer screen into audio output. The text should be a brief representation of the purpose of the image, not a description of the image, with the goal

More About

Images

Images on Web pages are viewed in a variety of environments, including slow connections to the Internet and slower computers. Optimizing your images is important to increase the speed of download for all of your Web page visitors. Visit the HTML More About Web page (scsite.com/html3e/more) and then click Optimization.

of helping those who cannot see the image use the site most effectively. Although the text can be any length, you generally should stick to 50 characters or less to avoid the browser wrapping the text. <img> tag attributes will be explained in detail as they are used in later projects. The width and height attributes will define the image size. It is important to include the height and width attributes so the browser knows the size of the image without having to calculate it.

Table 2-3 Image Attributes	
ATTRIBUTE	**FUNCTION**
align	• Controls alignment • Can select from bottom, middle, top, left, or right
alt	• Alternative text to display when an image is being loaded
border	• Defines the border width
height	• Defines the height of the image • Improves loading time
hspace	• Defines the horizontal space that separates the image from the text
src	• Defines the URL of the image to be loaded
vspace	• Defines the vertical space that separates the image from the text
width	• Defines the width of the image • Improves loading time

Improving the Appearance of Your Web Page

One goal in Web page development is to create a Web page that is visually appealing and maintains the interest of the visitors. The Web page developed thus far in the project is functional, but lacks in visual appeal. The following steps illustrate how to improve the appearance of the Web page from the one shown in Figure 2-25a to the one shown in Figure 2-25b by adding an image, adding a background color, centering a heading, and adding a horizontal rule.

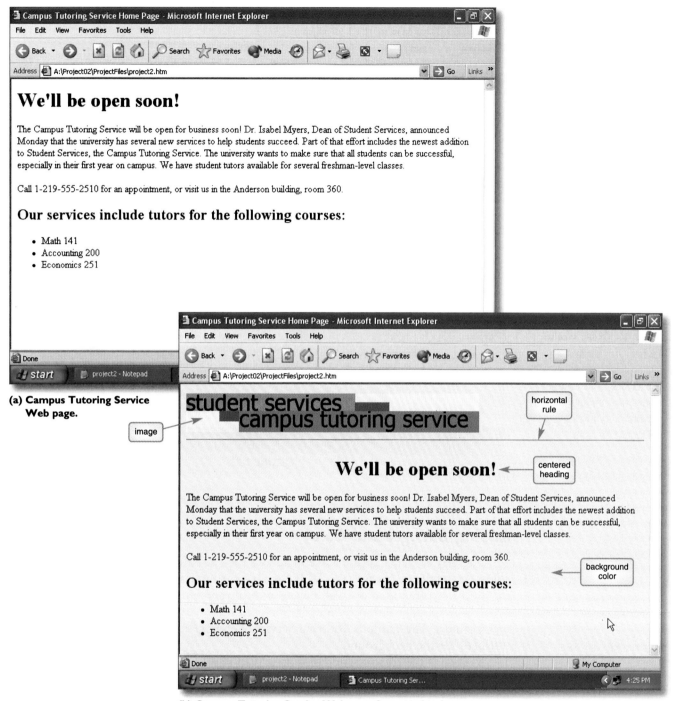

(a) Campus Tutoring Service Web page.

(b) Campus Tutoring Service Web page formatted to improve appearance.

FIGURE 2-25

Adding an Image

Early in the use of the Web, when the Web was used mostly by researchers needing to share information with each other, having purely functional, text-only Web pages was the norm. Today, however, the Web also serves as a communications and advertising medium, competing with television, radio, and print. Web page visitors are used to a more graphically oriented world. Because of this, Web page visitors have come to expect Web pages to use images that provide visual interest. The steps on the next page illustrate how to add an image to a Web page by entering an <img> tag in the HTML file.

To Add an Image

1

• **Click after the > symbol on line 10 and then press the ENTER key.**

2

• **Type** <img src="cts_clip8.gif" width="484" height="62" alt="Student Services logo" /> as the tag.

The HTML code inserts an image with the file name cts_clip8.gif (Figure 2-26). Because the image only uses a few colors, a GIF image provides high enough quality. For a more complex image, a JPEG would be used.

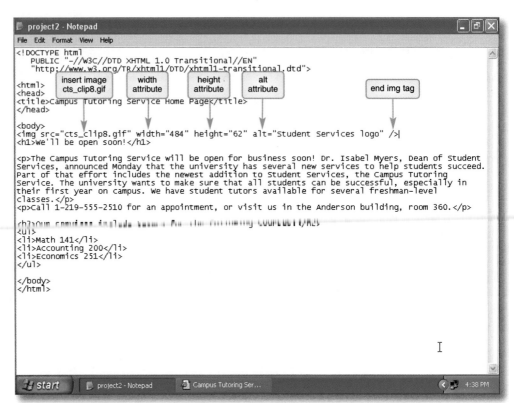

FIGURE 2-26

Adding Background Color

One way to help capture a Web page visitor's attention is to use color. Many colors are available for use as a Web page background, text, or link. Figure 2-27 shows colors often used on Web pages, with the corresponding six-digit number codes. The six-digit number codes can be used to specify a color for a background, text, or links. The Campus Tutoring Service Web page uses a pale yellow color (#fffbc6) for the background.

To change the background color on a Web page, the bgcolor attribute must be added in the <body> tag of the HTML file. The **bgcolor** attribute lets you change the background color of the Web page. The following steps show how to add a background color using the bgcolor attribute.

Q: Can I use a six-digit number code or color name to specify a background color?

A: Yes. You can use a six-digit number code or a color name as a background color choice. Figure 2-27 lists several predefined color names that can be used for background or font colors. The HTML attribute, background="navy", uses one of the predefined color choices.

COLORS IN HEX

Here is a table of common colors with their hexadecimal equivalents. Use the codes to define the desired color for the background, text, or links.

#FFC6A5	#FF9473	#FF6342	#FF3118	#FF0000	#D60000	#AD0000	#840000	#630000
#FFE7C6	#FFCE9C	#FFB573	#FF9C4A	#FF8429	#D66321	#AD4A18	#844D18	#632910
#FFFFC6	#FFFF9C	#FFFF6B	#FFFF42	#FFFF10	#D6C610	#AD9410	#847308	#635208
#F7FFCE	#EFEFAD	#E7F784	#DEF763	#D6EF39	#B5BD31	#8C9429	#6B6B21	#524A18
#DE93BD	#C6EF8C	#ADDE63	#94D639	#7BC618	#639C18	#527B10	#425A10	#314208
#CEEFBD	#A5DE94	#7BC66B	#52B552	#299C39	#218429	#186321	#184A18	#103910
#C6E7DE	#94D6CE	#63BDB5	#31ADA5	#089494	#087B7B	#006363	#004A4A	#003139
#C6EFF7	#94D6E7	#63C6DE	#31B5D6	#00A5C6	#0084A5	#006B84	#005263	#00394A
#BDC6DE	#949CCE	#6373B5	#3152A5	#083194	#082984	#08296B	#08215A	#00184A
#C6B5DE	#9C7BBD	#7B52A5	#522994	#31007B	#29006B	#21005A	#21004A	#180042
#DEBDDE	#CE84C6	#B552AD	#9C2994	#8C007B	#730063	#5A0052	#4A0042	#390031
#F7BDDE	#E78CC6	#DE5AAD	#D63194	#CE007B	#A50063	#840052	#6B0042	#520031
#FFFFFF	#E0E0E0	#BFBFBF	#A1A1A1	#808080	#616161	#404040	#212121	#000000

THE SIXTEEN PREDEFINED COLORS

(Because these colors belong to the RGB spectrum, they will look a bit different on-screen.)

Silver	Gray	Maroon	Green	Navy	Purple	Olive	Teal
White	Black	Red	Lime	Blue	Magenta	Yellow	Cyan

FIGURE 2-27 Common Web page colors.

More About

Colors

Figure 2-27 does not list all possible Web colors. Many other colors are available that you can use for Web page backgrounds or text fonts. For more information about colors, see Appendix B or visit the HTML More About Web page (scsite.com/html3e/more.htm) and then click Colors.

To Add a Background Color

1

• Click after the y in `<body>` on line 10 and then press the SPACEBAR.

2

• Type `bgcolor="#fffbc6"` as the color code.

The HTML code is displayed (Figure 2-28). The bgcolor attribute uses a six-digit number code of fffbc6 to specify a pale yellow background.

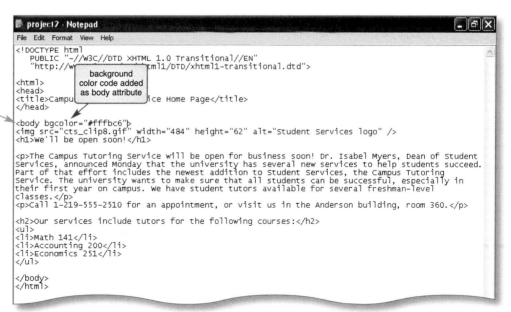

FIGURE 2-28

The color codes shown in Figure 2-27 on the previous page can be used for background, text, and link colors. The bgcolor attribute is used in the <body> tag to specify the background color for the Web page. In later projects, the text and link attributes are used in the <body> tag to change colors for those elements.

Centering the Heading

As discussed, headings are used to separate new sections of text from each other. A main heading is used to indicate the beginning of the Web page. Generally, you use the Heading 1 style for the main heading. The heading, We'll be open soon!, is the main heading and indicates the main message of the Web page. You can highlight the main heading further by aligning the text differently on the page. Using the **align** attribute, you can specify left-, right-, or center-alignment with the statements align="left", align="right", or align="center" in any heading tag. By default, headings are left-aligned; if an alignment is not specified, a heading is left-aligned. The following steps illustrate how to center align the heading.

To Center a Heading

1

• **Click line 12 just after the 1 in the <h1> tag and then press the SPACEBAR.**

2

• **Type** align="center" **as the attribute.**

The insertion point is positioned before the > symbol (Figure 2-29). The code to center-align the heading is added as a heading attribute.

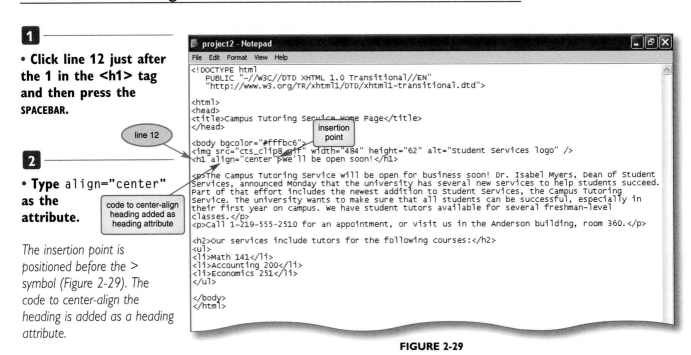

FIGURE 2-29

Adding a Horizontal Rule

As discussed earlier in the project, horizontal rules are lines that act as dividers in a Web page to provide a visual separation of sections on the page. You can use an inline image to add a horizontal rule or you can use the horizontal rule tag (<hr />) to add a simple horizontal rule, as shown in the steps below. Figure 2-30 shows examples of a variety of horizontal rules and the HTML code used to add them. The default horizontal rule is shown in the first line of the page. Dimension is added to a horizontal rule by increasing the number of pixels that are displayed. Another possibility is to turn the shading off using the noshade option, as shown in the last horizontal rule in Figure 2-30.

FIGURE 2-30 Examples of horizontal rules.

The following steps illustrate how to add a horizontal rule to a Web page.

To Add a Horizontal Rule

1 Click line 11 just after the > symbol in the **<img>** tag and then press the ENTER key.

2 Type **<hr />** as the HTML tag.

3 Click **File** on the menu bar and then click **Save**.

The project2 - Notepad window is displayed (Figure 2-31).

```
project2 - Notepad
File  Edit  Format  View  Help

<!DOCTYPE html
    PUBLIC "-//W3C//DTD XHTML 1.0 Transitional//EN"
    "http://www.w3.org/TR/xhtml1/DTD/xhtml1-transitional.dtd">

<html>
<head>
<title>Campus Tutoring Service Home Page</title>
</head>

<body bgcolor="#fff|                  th="484" height="62" alt="Student Services logo" />
<img src="cts_clip8
<hr />|
<h1 align="center">we'll be open soon!</h1>

<p>The Campus Tutoring Service will be open for business soon! Dr. Isabel Myers, Dean of Student
Services, announced Monday that the university has several new services to help students succeed.
Part of that effort includes the newest addition to Student Services, the Campus Tutoring
Service. The university wants to make sure that all students can be successful, especially in
their first year on campus. We have student tutors available for several freshman-level
classes.</p>
<p>Call 1-219-555-2510 for an appointment, or visit us in the Anderson building, room 360.</p>

<h2>Our services include tutors for the following courses:</h2>
<ul>
<li>Math 141</li>
<li>Accounting 200</li>
<li>Economics 251</li>
</ul>

</body>
</html>
```

insertion point

horizontal rule tag

Campus Tutoring Service Home Page button

FIGURE 2-31

Refreshing the View in a Browser

After you have saved the modifications to the HTML file, the modified Web page can be viewed in a browser to review the background color, inserted image, centered heading, and horizontal rule. To view the latest version of the Web page in a browser, the page must be reloaded, or refreshed. The following steps show how to refresh the view of a Web page in a browser in order to view the modified Web page.

To Refresh the View in a Browser

1

• **Click the Campus Tutoring Service Home Page button on the taskbar.**

2

• **Click the Refresh button on the Standard toolbar.**

The latest version of project2.htm is displayed (Figure 2-32).

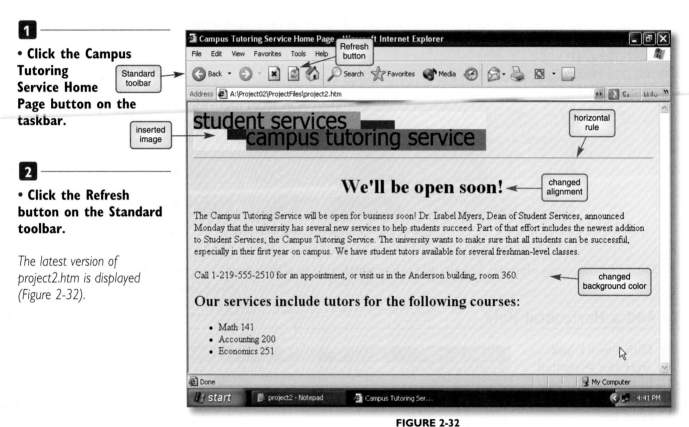

FIGURE 2-32

As discussed earlier in the project, Windows supports multitasking, so you can have Notepad and your browser open at the same time. You can continue developing the HTML file in Notepad and then view the modified file in your browser by clicking the appropriate button on the taskbar to switch between Notepad and the browser. Be sure to click the Refresh button when viewing the modified Web page in the browser, to ensure the latest version of the Web page is displayed.

Viewing HTML Source Code for a Web Page

Source code is the code or instructions used to create a Web page or program. For a Web page, the source code is the HTML code, which then is translated by a browser into a graphical Web page. You can view the HTML source code for any Web page from within your browser. This feature allows you to check your own HTML source code, as well as to see the HTML code other developers used to create their Web pages. If a feature on a Web page is appropriate or appealing for your Web page, you can view the source to understand the HTML required to add that feature and then copy sections of the HTML code to put in your own Web pages.

The following steps show how to view the HTML source code for a Web page using a browser.

To View HTML Source Code for a Web Page

1

• **Click View on the menu bar (Figure 2-33).**

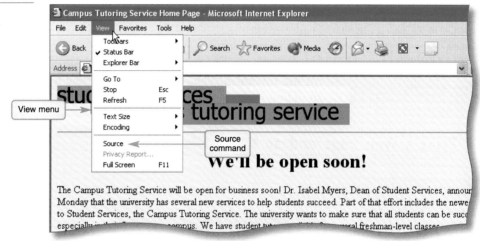

FIGURE 2-33

2

• **Click Source on the View menu.**

A Notepad window opens and displays the HTML source code for the Web page (Figure 2-34).

3

• **Click the Close button on the Notepad title bar.**

The Notepad window closes.

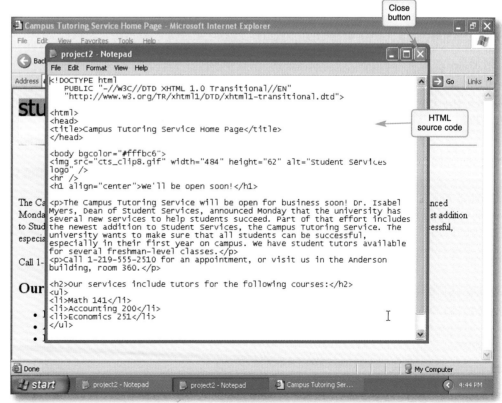

FIGURE 2-34

The HTML source code opens in the default text editor when you view the source. Although one Notepad window already was open, clicking View and then Source opened a second Notepad window.

Printing a Web Page and an HTML File

After you have created the HTML file and saved it, you might want to print a copy of the HTML code and the resulting Web page. A printed version of a file, Web page, or other document is called a **hard copy** or **printout**.

Printouts are used for several reasons. Printouts allow you to present information to someone who does not have immediate access to a computer. A printout, for example, can be handed out in a meeting at which you are discussing sample Web pages. In addition, printed copies of HTML files and Web pages can be kept for reference. In many cases, HTML files and Web pages are printed and kept in binders for use by others. The following steps show how to print a Web page and its corresponding HTML file.

> ### More About
>
> **Printing HTML Files and Web Pages**
>
> Notepad and Internet Explorer both provide other ways to print a document or Web page. Pressing CTRL + P in Notepad or Internet Explorer opens the Print dialog box, where you can select print options. Alternatively, you can print a Web page in Internet Explorer by clicking the Print button on the Standard Buttons toolbar.

To Print a Web Page and an HTML File

1

• **Ready the printer according to the printer instructions.**

• **With the project2.htm Web page open in the browser window, click File on the menu bar and then click Print on the File menu.**

• **Click the OK button in the Print dialog box.**

2

• **When the printer stops printing the Web page, retrieve the printout (Figure 2-35).**

3

• **Click the Notepad button on the taskbar to activate the Notepad window.**

---

student services
campus tutoring service

We'll be open soon!

The Campus Tutoring Service will be open for business soon! Dr. Isabel Myers, Dean of Student Services, announced Monday that the university has several new services to help students succeed. Part of that effort includes the newest addition to Student Services, the Campus Tutoring Service. The university wants to make sure that all students can be successful, especially in their first year on campus. We have student tutors available for several freshman-level classes.

Call 1-219-555-2510 for an appointment, or visit us in the Anderson building, room 360.

Our services include tutors for the following courses:

- Math 141
- Accounting 200
- Economics 251

FIGURE 2-35

4

• **Click File on the menu bar and then click Print on the File menu.**

Notepad prints the HTML file (Figure 2-36).

```
<!DOCTYPE html
    PUBLIC "-//W3C//DTD XHTML 1.0 Transitional//EN"
    "http://www.w3.org/TR/xhtml1/DTD/xhtml1-transitional.dtd">

<html>
<head>
<title>Campus Tutoring Service Home Page</title>
</head>

<body bgcolor="#fffbc6">
<img src="cts_clip8.gif">
<hr />
<h1 align="center">We'll be open soon!</h1>

<p>The Campus Tutoring Service will be open for business soon! Dr. Isabel Myers,
Dean of Student

Services, announced Monday that the university has several new services to help
students succeed.

Part of that effort includes the newest addition to Student Services, the Campus
Tutoring

Service. The university wants to make sure that all students can be successful,
especially in

their first year on campus. We have student tutors available for several
freshman-level

classes.</p>
<p>Call 1-219-555-2510 for an appointment, or visit us in the Anderson building,
room 360.</p>

<h2>Our services include tutors for the following courses:</h2>
<ul>
<li>Math 141</li>
<li>Accounting 200</li>
<li>Economics 251</li>
</ul>

</body>
</html>
```

FIGURE 2-36

Having a printout of HTML code is an invaluable tool for beginning developers. A printed copy can help you immediately see the relationship between the HTML tags and the Web page that you view in the browser.

Quitting Notepad and a Browser

The following steps show how to quit Notepad and a browser.

To Quit Notepad and a Browser

- **Click the Close button on the Notepad title bar.**

The Notepad window closes and the Campus Tutoring Service Home Page window is displayed.

- **Click the Close button on the Campus Tutoring Service Home Page title bar.**

The browser closes and the Windows desktop is displayed.

Project Summary

Project 2 introduced the steps to start Notepad and create an HTML text file. You learned about the elements of a Web page and the HTML tags used to add those elements. You learned how to enter HTML tags and text using Notepad and then save the file. After learning how to view a Web page in a browser, you learned to modify the HTML file to improve the Web page appearance by using an image, adding a background color, centering a heading, and adding a horizontal rule. You then learned to refresh the view of the Web page in the browser to see the changes. Finally, you learned how to save the changes, print the Web page and HTML file, and quit Notepad and the browser.

What You Should Know

Having completed this project, you should be able to perform the tasks below. The tasks are listed in the same order they were presented in this project.

1. Start Notepad (HTM 34)
2. Enable Word Wrap in Notepad (HTM 36)
3. Enter HTML Tags to Define the Web Page Structure (HTM 38)
4. Enter a Heading (HTM 40)
5. Enter a Paragraph of Text (HTM 40)
6. Create an Unordered List (HTM 43)
7. Save an HTML File (HTM 45)
8. Start a Browser (HTM 47)
9. View a Web Page in a Browser (HTM 49)
10. Activate Notepad (HTM 50)
11. Add an Image (HTM 54)
12. Add a Background Color (HTM 55)
13. Center a Heading (HTM 56)
14. Add a Horizontal Rule (HTM 57)
15. Refresh the View in a Browser (HTM 58)
16. View HTML Source Code for a Web Page (HTM 59)
17. Print a Web Page and an HTML File (HTM 60)
18. Quit Notepad and a Browser (HTM 62)

Learn It Online

Instructions: To complete the Learn It Online exercises, start your browser, click the Address bar, and then enter the Web address scsite.com/html3e/learn. When the HTML Learn It Online page is displayed, follow the instructions in the exercises below. Each exercise has instructions for printing your results, either for your own records or for submission to your instructor.

1 Project Reinforcement TF, MC, and SA

Below HTML Project 2, click the Project Reinforcement link. Print the quiz by clicking Print on the File menu for each page. Answer each question.

2 Flash Cards

Below HTML Project 2, click the Flash Cards link and read the instructions. Type 20 (or a number specified by your instructor) in the Number of playing cards text box, type your name in the Enter your Name text box, and then click the Flip Card button. When the flash card is displayed, read the question and then click the ANSWER box arrow to select an answer. Flip through Flash Cards. If your score is 15 (75%) correct or greater, click Print on the File menu to print your results. If your score is less than 15 (75%) correct, then redo this exercise by clicking the Replay button.

3 Practice Test

Below HTML Project 2, click the Practice Test link. Answer each question, enter your first and last name at the bottom of the page, and then click the Grade Test button. When the graded practice test is displayed on your screen, click Print on the File menu to print a hard copy. Continue to take practice tests until you score 80% or better.

4 Who Wants To Be a Computer Genius?

Below HTML Project 2, click the Computer Genius link. Read the instructions, enter your first and last name at the bottom of the page, and then click the PLAY button. When your score is displayed, click the PRINT RESULTS link to print a hard copy.

5 Wheel of Terms

Below HTML Project 2, click the Wheel of Terms link. Read the instructions, and then enter your first and last name and your school name. Click the PLAY button. When your score is displayed, right-click the score and then click Print on the shortcut menu to print a hard copy.

6 Crossword Puzzle Challenge

Below HTML Project 2, click the Crossword Puzzle Challenge link. Read the instructions, and then enter your first and last name. Click the SUBMIT button. Work the crossword puzzle. When you are finished, click the Submit button. When the crossword puzzle is redisplayed, click the Print Puzzle button to print a hard copy.

7 Tips and Tricks

Below HTML Project 2, click the Tips and Tricks link. Click a topic that pertains to Project 2. Right-click the information and then click Print on the shortcut menu. Construct a brief example of what the information relates to in HTML to confirm you understand how to use the tip or trick.

8 Newsgroups

Below HTML Project 2, click the Newsgroups link. Click a topic that pertains to Project 2. Print three comments.

9 Expanding Your Horizons

Below HTML Project 2, click the Expanding Your Horizons link. Click a topic that pertains to Project 2. Print the information. Construct a brief example of what the information relates to in HTML to confirm you understand the contents of the article.

10 Search Sleuth

Below HTML Project 2, click the Search Sleuth link. To search for a term that pertains to this project, select a term below the Project 2 title and then use the Google search engine at google.com (or any major search engine) to display and print two Web pages that present information on the term.

11 Online Help I

Below HTML Project 2, click the Online Help I link. Follow the instructions on the page to access Web pages that provide additional help on project topics. Hand in any printed information to your instructor.

12 Online Help II

Below HTML Project 2, click the Online Help II link. Follow the instructions on the page to access Web pages that provide additional help on project topics. Hand in any printed information to your instructor.

1 Editing the Apply Your Knowledge Web Page

Instructions: Start Notepad. Open the file, apply2-1.htm, from the Project02\AYK folder on the HTML Data Disk. If you did not download the HTML Data Disk, see the inside back cover for instructions or see your instructor. The apply2-1.htm file is a partially completed HTML file that contains some errors. Figure 2-37 shows the Apply Your Knowledge Web page as it should be displayed in a browser after the errors are corrected.

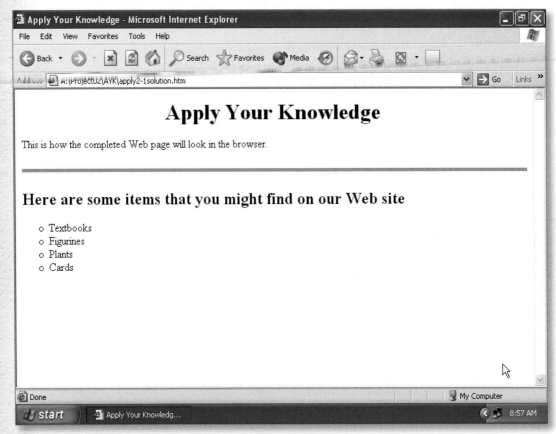

FIGURE 2-37

Perform the following steps using a computer:

1. Enter a:\Project02\AYK\apply2-1.htm as the URL to view the Web page in your browser.
2. Examine the HTML file and its appearance in the browser.
3. Use Notepad to open the file, apply2-1.htm, from the Project02\AYK folder on the HTML Data Disk. Correct the HTML errors, making the Web page look similar to the one shown in Figure 2-37.
4. Add any HTML code necessary for additional features shown in the Web page.
5. Save the revised HTML file in the Project02\AYK folder on the HTML Data Disk using the file name apply2-1solution.htm.
6. Print the revised HTML file.
7. Enter a:\Project02\AYK\apply2-1solution.htm as the URL to view the revised Web page in your browser.
8. Print the Web page.
9. Write your name on both printouts and hand them in to your instructor.

1 Creating a Personal Web Page

Problem: Your instructor would like to create a Web page that lists key Internet concepts and make the Web page available on the World Wide Web. You have been asked to create a Web page to display this information, similar to the one shown in Figure 2-38.

FIGURE 2-38

Instructions: Start Notepad. Perform the following steps using a computer:

1. Start a new HTML file with the title, [Your Name] LAB2-1, in the main heading section.
2. Begin the body section by adding the heading, Internet Concepts. Format the heading to use the Heading 1 style and be centered on the Web page.
3. Add a horizontal rule below the Internet Concepts heading.
4. Add two headings, Key Terms and Web Page Elements, using the Heading 2 style.
5. Add two ordered lists of topics as shown in Figure 2-38.
6. Save the HTML file in the Project02\IntheLab folder on the HTML Data Disk using the file name lab2-1.htm.
7. Print the lab2-1.htm file.
8. Enter a:\Project02\IntheLab\lab2-1.htm as the URL to view the Web page in your browser.
9. Print the Web page.
10. Write your name on the printouts and hand them in to your instructor.

2 Creating an Information Web Page

Problem: You are the president of the academic honor society, Phi Kappa Phi, and decide to prepare a Web page announcement, such as the one shown in Figure 2-39, to share the club's history and to invite new members to join the club.

FIGURE 2-39

Instructions: Start Notepad. Perform the following steps using a computer:

1. Start a new HTML file with the title [Your Name] LAB2-2 in the main heading section.
2. Add a colored background to the Web page using the #ffffcc color code.
3. Begin the body section by adding the heading, Phi Kappa Phi. Format the heading to use the Heading 1 style and be center-aligned on the Web page.
4. Add a size 10 horizontal rule with noshade below the heading.
5. Add a heading, Main Topics, using a left-aligned Heading 2 style.
6. Add a paragraph of text, as shown in Figure 2-39.
7. Add a size 10 horizontal rule with noshade below the paragraph.
8. Save the HTML file in the Project02\IntheLab folder on the HTML Data Disk using the file name lab2-2.htm.
9. Print the lab2-2.htm file.
10. Enter `a:\Project02\IntheLab\lab2-2.htm` as the URL to view the Web page in your browser.
11. Print the Web page.
12. Write your name on the printouts and hand them in to your instructor.

3 Composing a Personal Web Page

Problem: Your manager at Student Services asked you to create a personal Web page to tell people about yourself, your experience tutoring students, and why you think using the Campus Tutoring Service can be beneficial for students. You plan to use paragraphs of text and a bulleted list, as shown in Figure 2-40.

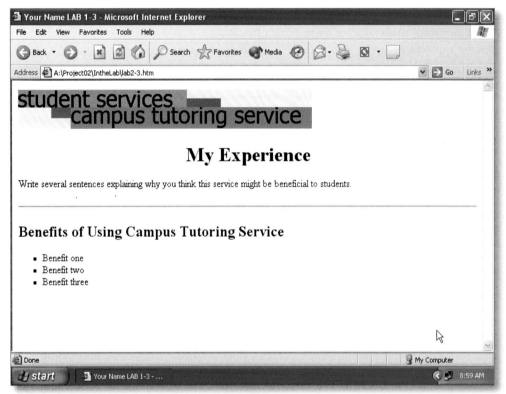

FIGURE 2-40

Instructions: Start Notepad. Perform the following steps using a computer:

1. Start a new HTML file with the title [your name] lab2-3 in the main heading section.
2. Include a short paragraph of information and a bulleted list, using a format similar to the one shown in Figure 2-40, to provide information about your tutoring experience.
3. Save the HTML file in the Project02\IntheLab folder on the HTML Data Disk using the file name lab2-3.htm.
4. Enter `a:\Project02\IntheLab\lab2-3.htm` as the URL to view the Web page in your browser.
5. Print the Web page from your browser.
6. Write your name on the printout and hand it in to your instructor.

Cases and Places

The difficulty of these case studies varies:
■ are the least difficult and ■■ are the most difficult. The last exercise is a group exercise.

1 ■ Dr. Meyers likes the Campus Tutoring Service Web page created in Project 2. Now that the Campus Tutoring Service is open, she would like you to update it with new information on available tutors and hours of availability. Before updating the page, search the Web to review the student services and tutoring services Web pages at other schools and universities for ideas on content to include or formatting to change. What do their Web sites look like? Are there changes you can make to the Project 2 Web page that reflect what other schools have done? Using the concepts presented in this project, include additional information or change the formatting to make the page more interesting and timely.

2 ■ Your class instructor wants to post all of the students' Web pages on the school server to show what her students have learned in class. Create a Web page of personal information, listing items such as your school major, jobs that you have had in the past, and your hobbies and interests. In order to make your personal Web page more visually interesting, search the Web for images that reflect your interests (be sure that the image is not copyrighted or you cannot use it on a personal Web page). Insert an image or two onto the Web page to help explain who you are.

3 ■■ As an instructor at NewCourses training, you often update your Web site with information to help students in your classes. For an upcoming HTML class, you have decided to create a Web page with a definition list of HTML tags and their usage. Using the concepts presented in this project, use Notepad to create a Web page with the information listed in Table 2-1 on page HTM 37. Add the heading, HTML Tags and Their Functions, at the top of the page. Use the HTML tag as the term (<dt>) and function as the definition of the term (<dd>).

4 ■■ You are creating a new Web site for a local KidDayz childcare center. The director of the center has asked that you use descriptive alt attributes for images on the Web page, as the parents of many of the children have very slow Internet connections and images often do not load quickly. Search the Web for information on adding useful, descriptive alt attributes for images. Create a document with a brief paragraph explaining the various purposes of alt attributes. Include three examples of good, descriptive alt attributes and three examples of less descriptive alt attributes.

5 ■■ **Working Together** You are part of a Web usability team for Axcelent, a local Web design firm. As part of a new project on the use of color on the Web, your team is doing research on which background colors are more appealing to users. Search the Web for information about browser-safe colors on the Web. Create three Web pages with the same information but vary the background color. Be sure to save each different page as a different file name. Show those pages to some friends or family members to have them evaluate which color of background they like and explain why they prefer one color to another. View these three Web pages on different computers used by members of the team. Do the colors look different? Why do you think they would? What factors contribute to the way in which a colored background would be displayed?

Creating Web Pages with Links, Images, and Formatted Text

CASE PERSPECTIVE

Plant World is a local nursery that specializes in landscape design and the sale of indoor and outdoor plants at its 38 New England store locations. You want to advance your current company position by using the knowledge you gained from recently finishing an HTML course. You can envision developing Web pages that advertise the company to current and prospective customers and help promote specific types of plants, by providing information on planting and seasonal care.

You know that, once you have some sample Web pages to show your boss, Jared Smith, you will be able to convince him that this idea will offer the company Internet exposure and a marketing presence on the Web. With this in mind, you develop two Web pages using HTML. The first Web page includes information about Plant World, a link to a second Web page, and an e-mail link to the company e-mail address. The second Web page includes information on several different types of plants, as well as a link to a Web page with additional information. Because it is long, you also used links within the second Web page to make it easier to navigate. After these Web pages are completed, you plan to take them to Jared to explain your idea.

In this project, you will learn how to use Notepad to create, save, and print an HTML file to create a Web page, as well as to open and edit an existing HTML file. You also will learn how to use different types of links, including an e-mail link, a text link and an image link to a second Web page, internal links to navigate within a single Web page, and an external link to a different Web site. Finally, you will learn to add a background image, wrap text around an image, and format text using bold, italic, and colored fonts.

Creating Web Pages with Links, Images, and Formatted Text

Introduction

As you have learned, hyperlinks, or links, are an essential part of the World Wide Web, allowing developers to connect one Web page to another Web page on the same, or a different, Web server located anywhere in the world. Using hyperlinks, a Web site visitor can move from one page to another, to view information in any order. Many different Web page elements, including text, graphics, and animations, can serve as hyperlinks.

In this project, you will learn how to create Web pages using the following types of links:

- text and image links to another Web page in the same Web site
- text links to another Web page in a different Web site
- text links within a Web page
- e-mail links

You also will learn to add a background image and bulleted (unordered) lists to a Web page. After learning how to open an existing HTML file in Notepad, you will learn to write HTML code to insert and wrap text around an image and to format text using bold, italics, and colored fonts. Finally, you will learn to view the Web pages, test the links, and then print the HTML code and the Web page.

Project Three — Plant World Web Site

Project 3 illustrates how to use HTML to create a home page for the Plant World Web site (Figure 3-1a) and to edit the existing Desert Plants Web page (Figure 3-1b) to improve the appearance and function. The Plant World home page, which displays information about Plant World and its services, includes a logo image, headings, two unordered (bulleted) lists, an e-mail link, and a link to the Desert Plants Web page. The Desert Plants Web page contains images with text wrapped around them and internal links that allow visitors to move easily from section to section within the Web page. This page also includes a text link to a Web page on another Web site and an image link back to Plant World's home page. The basic HTML for the Desert Plants Web page is included on the HTML Data Disk.

image link back to home page

(a) Plant World home page.

link to Desert Plants Web page

e-mail link

(c) Linked Web page in external Web site.

text link to external Web site

(b) Desert Plants Web page.

FIGURE 3-1

Starting Notepad

The first step in creating a home page for the Plant World Web site is to start Notepad. The following steps show how to start Notepad and maximize the window.

To Start Notepad

1 Click the Start button on the taskbar and then point to All Programs on the Start menu.

2 Point to Accessories on the All Programs submenu and then point to Notepad on the Accessories submenu.

3 Click Notepad.

4 If the Notepad window is not maximized, click the Maximize button on the Notepad title bar to maximize it.

5 Click Format on the menu bar.

6 If Word Wrap is not checked, click Word Wrap.

The Notepad window is displayed and Word Wrap is enabled.

More About

Link Help

Many World Wide Web sites provide help for new HTML developers. For more information about links, visit the HTML More About Web page (scsite.com/html3e/more.htm) and then click Link Help.

Using Links on a Web Page

As you have learned, many different Web page elements, including text, images, and animations, can serve as links. Text and images are the elements most widely used as links. Figure 3-2 shows an example of a text link, and Figure 3-3 shows an example of an image link. Generally, moving the mouse pointer over a link causes the mouse pointer to change to a pointing hand. This change notifies the user that a link is available from that text or image. As shown in Figure 3-2, moving the mouse pointer over a link also displays the URL of the linked page, document, or other file on the status bar of the browser.

FIGURE 3-2 Text link on Web page.

FIGURE 3-3 Image link on Web page.

When using text links on a Web page, use descriptive text as the clickable word or phrase. For example, the phrase, Click here, does not explain the purpose of the link to the visitor. By contrast, the phrase, Save up to 60% on airfare, indicates that the link connects to a Web page with discounted airline tickets. As shown in Figure 3-2, when text identifies a link, it often appears as underlined text, in a color different from the rest of the Web page text.

Unless otherwise coded in the <body> tag, the browser settings define the colors of text links throughout a Web page. For example, with Internet Explorer, the default color for a normal link that has not been clicked (or visited) is blue, a visited link is purple, and an active link (a link just clicked by a user) is green. Figure 3-4 shows examples of text links in all three states (normal, visited, and active).

> **More About**
>
> ### Linking Colors
>
> You can change the link colors in popular browsers. In Microsoft Internet Explorer, you find color selection on the Tools menu using Internet Options. In Netscape Communicator, click Preferences on the Edit menu. In both products, you change colors by clicking the color bars.

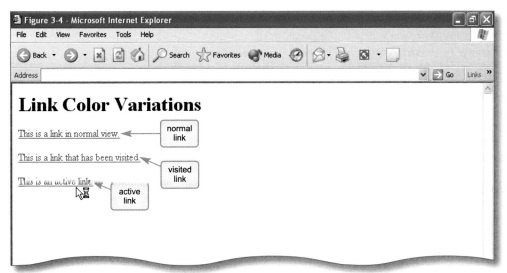

FIGURE 3-4 Examples of text link color variations.

The same color defaults apply to the border color around an image link. A border makes the image display as if it has a frame around it, as shown in Figure 3-5. If the image has no border, no color will display around the image. If the image has a border but is not used as a link, the border displays in black, as shown in the left image in Figure 3-5. If the image is used as a link, the default link colors display as the image border when the link is normal, active, or visited. The center image in Figure 3-5 shows an image with a border, which is used as a link. The link displays in the default color, which indicates it has not been clicked (visited). The image on the right in Figure 3-5 shows the changed border color after the link has been visited, giving the image an entirely different look.

FIGURE 3-5 Examples of image border and link color variations.

If you want to change the colors of text links or image link borders to override the browser defaults, you must enter attributes and values in the <body> tag. The format of the tag used to change normal, visited, and active link colors from the default is

```
<body link="color" vlink="color" alink="color">
```

where color is a designated color code, such as #6633CC. Table 3-1 lists the link color attributes that can be specified in the <body> tag.

Table 3-1 Link Color Attributes for <body> Tag

ATTRIBUTE	FUNCTION
link	• Normal link • Controls the color of a normal unvisited link and/or link without mouse pointer pointing to it • Default color usually is blue
vlink	• Visited link • Controls the color of a link that has been clicked or visited • Default color usually is green or purple
alink	• Active link • Controls the color of a link immediately after the mouse clicks the hyperlink • Default color usually is green or red

Linking to Another Web Page within the Same Web Site

Web pages often include links to connect one Web page to another page within the same Web site. For example, a visitor can click a link on the home page of a Web site (Figure 3-6a) to connect and view another Web page on the same Web site (Figure 3-6b). Links between pages on a Web site allow visitors to move from one Web page to another, in a Web site with multiple pages. The Web pages created in this project include links to other pages in the same Web site: (1) the Plant World home page includes a text link to the Desert Plants Web page and (2) the Desert Plants Web page includes an image link to the Plant World home page.

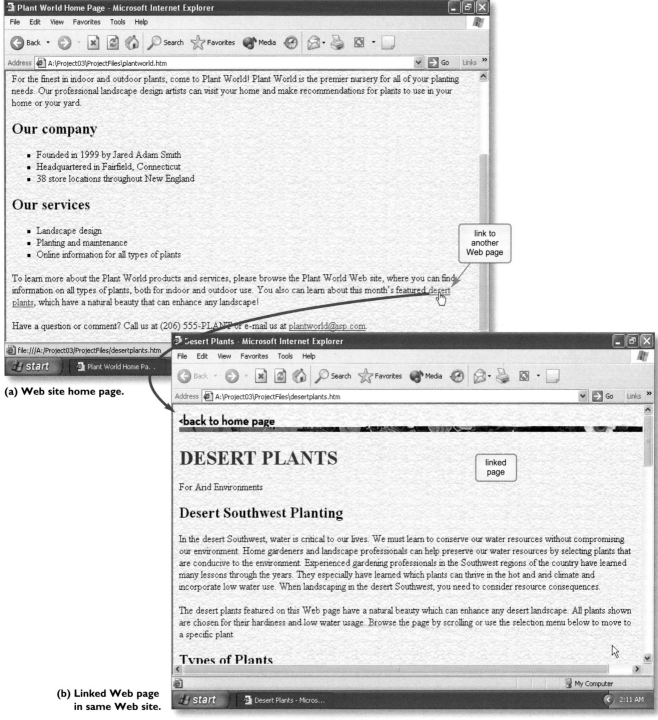

(a) Web site home page.

(b) Linked Web page in same Web site.

FIGURE 3-6

Linking to a Web Page in Another Web Site

A very important feature of the Web is the capability of linking a Web page on one Web site to a Web page on another external Web site. Web developers use these links to connect their Web pages to other Web pages with information on the same topic. In this project, the Desert Plants Web page (Figure 3-7a) includes a link to a page on another Web site, where the visitor can find additional desert plant information. (Figure 3-7b).

(a) **Web page with text link to external Web site.**

(b) **Linked Web page in external Web site.**

FIGURE 3-7

Linking within a Web Page

Links within a Web page allow visitors to move quickly from one section of the Web page to another. This is especially important in Web pages that are long and require a visitor to scroll down to see all of the content. By including links within a Web page, a visitor can click a link to move directly to a section of interest, rather than scrolling through the entire Web page. Many Web pages contain a list of links like a menu or table of contents at the top of the page, with links to sections within the Web page (Figure 3-8). In this project, the Desert Plants Web page includes links from the top section of the Web page to other sections within the page, as well as links back to the top of the Web page.

More About

Links on a Web Page

An anchor tag also allows visitors to move within a single Web page. Use the name attribute to allow movement from one area to another on the same page. This linking technique is useful particularly on long pages. An index of links also can provide easy access to various areas within the Web page.

FIGURE 3-8 Web page with internal links.

Linking to an E-Mail Address

A well-designed Web page always provides a way for visitors to contact the person at the company responsible for maintaining the Web site or addressing customer questions and comments. An easy way to provide contact information is to include an e-mail link on the Web site's home page, as well as on other pages in the Web site. As shown in Figure 3-9 on the next page, when a visitor clicks the **e-mail link**, it automatically opens a new message in the default e-mail program and inserts the appropriate contact e-mail address in the To field. Visitors then can type and send an e-mail to request additional information, comment on the Web site, or notify the company of a problem with its Web site.

(a) Web page with e-mail link.

(b) New Message window.

FIGURE 3-9

Creating a Home Page

The first Web page developed in this project is the home page of the Plant World Web site. A home page is the main page of a Web site, which visitors to a Web site generally will view first. A Web site home page should identify the purpose of the Web site, by briefly stating what content, services, or features it provides. The home page also should indicate clearly what links the visitor should click to move from one Web page on the Web site to another. A Web developer should design the Web site in such a way that the links from one Web page to another are apparent and the navigation is clear. The Web site home page also should include an e-mail link, so visitors easily can find contact information for the individual or organization.

Entering HTML Tags to Define the Web Page Structure

As you have learned, every HTML file includes HTML tags that define the overall structure of a standard Web page and divide the HTML file into its basic sections. The following steps show how to enter the HTML tags that define the structure of the Plant World home page.

To Enter HTML Tags to Define the Web Page Structure

1 Type `<!DOCTYPE html` **and then press the ENTER key.**

2 Press the SPACEBAR **three times, type** `PUBLIC "-//W3C//DTD XHTML 1.0 Transitional//EN"` **as the entry, and then press the ENTER key.**

3 Press the SPACEBAR **three times, type** `"http://www.w3.org/TR/xhtml1/DTD/ xhtml1-transitional.dtd">` **as the entry, and then press the ENTER key twice.**

4 Type `<html>` **and then press the ENTER key.**

5 Type `<head>` **and then press the ENTER key.**

6 Type `<title>Plant World Home Page</title>` **and then press the ENTER key.**

7 Type `</head>` **and then press the ENTER key.**

8 Type `<body>` **and then press the ENTER key twice.**

9 Type `</body>` **and then press the ENTER key.**

10 Type `</html>` **as the final tag.**

11 **Position the insertion on the blank line (line 10) between the <body> and </body> tags.**

The HTML code is displayed (Figure 3-10).

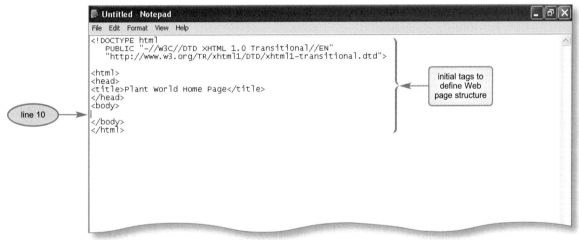

FIGURE 3-10

Adding an Image

Many Web developers utilize images to enhance the look of a Web page. In this project, the Plant World home page includes an image logo to provide visual appeal, catch the visitor's interest, and promote the company's brand. The logo image contains the name of the company and the city, state, and zip information. Often, a logo image on a company's Web site is the same image that is printed on company stationary, cards, and other promotional material distributed by the company. Using the same graphical image on all marketing materials, including the Web site, is a good way to provide a consistent visual and brand message to customers, so they connect your Web site with your product, signage, direct mail pieces, and so on.

As introduced in Project 2, the HTML tag used to include an image in a Web page also should include the width, height, and alt attributes. Identifying the width and height attributes can improve page loading time, because the browser does not have to determine the width and height of the image. The alt attribute displays as the Web page is loading and when a user moves the mouse over the image to provide additional information on the purpose of the image.

The following step illustrates how to add an image to a Web page by entering an <img> tag in the HTML file. The image file is stored on the HTML Data Disk. See the inside back cover for instructions for downloading the HTML Data Disk, or see your instructor.

To Add an Image

1

• **Type** <img src= "plantworldlg.jpg" width="720" height="84" alt="Plant World logo" /> **and then press the ENTER key.**

The HTML code inserts an image with the file name, plantworldlg.jpg (Figure 3-11).

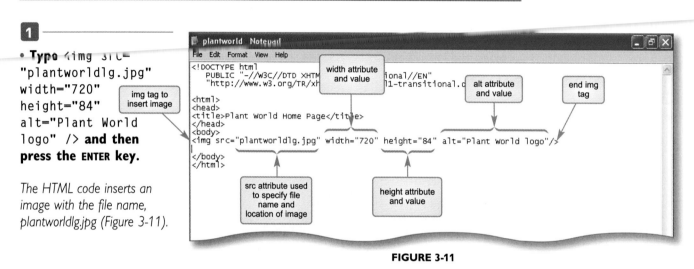

FIGURE 3-11

The attributes specified for the image indicate that the image is 720 pixels wide by 84 pixels high and will display the text, Plant World logo, when the mouse points to the image. Because the logo image uses photo elements, it is added as a JPEG image, which supports more colors and resolutions than GIF or PNG images.

Adding a Left-Aligned Heading with a Font Color

As discussed in Project 2, the <h1> tag assigns the largest possible size to a heading. Using the align attribute of the heading tag, you can specify left-, right-, or center-alignment with the statements align="left", align ="right", or align ="center". By default, headings are left-aligned, which means that, if an alignment is not specified, the heading will be left-aligned. The design of the Plant World home page makes it appropriate to left-align the heading on the Web page. Because the heading will be left-aligned, you do not have to specify an align attribute and value in the <h1> tag.

Text can be formatted using different colors and styles to make it stand out further on a Web page. Any text on a Web page, including headings, can be formatted with a different color or style by using attributes of the <font> tag. Table 3-2 lists the different font attributes that can be used to enhance standard text on a Web page.

ATTRIBUTE AND VALUE	FUNCTION
color="#xxxxxx"	• Changes the font color • Value inside quotation marks is a six-digit color code or color name
face="fontname"	• Changes the font face or type • Value inside quotation marks is the name of a font, such as Verdana or Arial; text appears using the default font if the font face is not specified
size="x"	• Changes the font size • Value inside quotation marks is a number that represents size • Values can be an actual font size of 1 (smallest) to 7 (largest) or a relative font size, such as +2 or -1, which specifies a number of sizes larger or smaller than the preset font size

Table 3-2 Font Attributes and Values

Q: What if a Web page uses a font visitors do not have on their computers?

A: If a Web page uses a font that Web page visitors do not have on their computers, the Web page appears using a default font (usually Times New Roman). If you want a heading with a specific font, create the heading as a graphic using the desired font.

Figure 3-12 lists several of these attributes and how they affect the text.

FIGURE 3-12 Examples of various font attributes.

The following step shows how to enter HTML code to add a left-aligned heading formatted in color to provide visual impact.

To Add a Left-Aligned Heading with a Font Color

1

• **With the insertion point on line 11, type** `<h1><font color="#000066">Welcome to Plant World!</font></h1>` **and then press the ENTER key.**

The HTML code for the heading is displayed (Figure 3-13). The color attribute uses a six-digit number code of #000066 to specify that the heading should appear in a navy blue color.

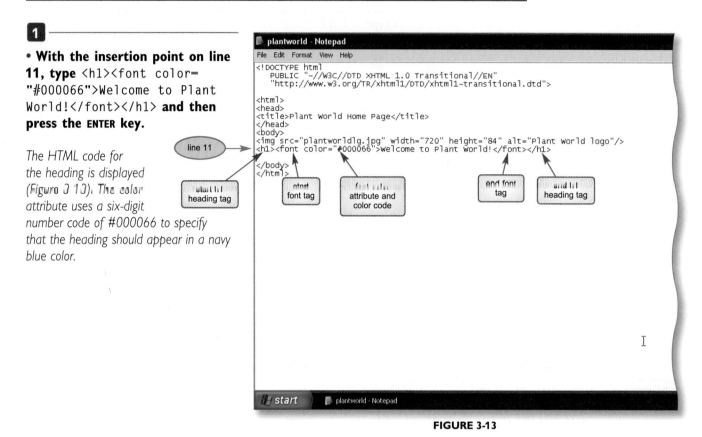

FIGURE 3-13

For additional color options, reference Figure 2-27 on page HTM 55 to see the list of possible color codes and names.

As discussed in Project 1, XHTML coding standards require that tags be nested properly. Nesting tags properly means that you always must enter end tags in an order opposite from the start tags. For example, as shown in Figure 3-13, the HTML code started with the start <h1> heading tag, followed by the start <font> tag. The end tags thus must be entered in the opposite order, with the end </font> tag first, followed by the end </h1> heading tag. This technique is similar to math equations.

Entering a Paragraph of Text

After the heading for the Plant World home page is entered, a paragraph of Web page text introducing Plant World can be entered. The following steps illustrate how to enter a paragraph of text in an HTML file.

More About

Font Sizes

The most frequently used font attribute is size. The values of font sizes range from 1 to 7, with 3 being the default. You also can specify the font size as a relative value using a + (plus) or – (minus) sign. These relative values range from –3 to +4.

To Enter a Paragraph of Text

1 **With the insertion point on line 12, type** `<p>For the finest in indoor and outdoor plants, come to Plant World! Plant World is the premier nursery for all of your planting needs. Our professional landscape design artists can visit your home and make recommendations for plants to use in your home or your yard.</p>` **as the first paragraph in the HTML file.**

2 **Press the ENTER key twice.**

The paragraph text is displayed in the HTML file (Figure 3-14).

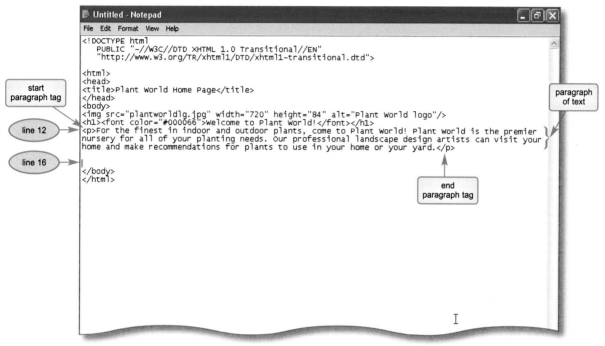

FIGURE 3-14

Creating Unordered (Bulleted) Lists

In Project 2, you learned how to create an unordered (bulleted) list on a Web page. Because the HTML code for the list did not specify a bullet type, the list used the default disc bullet. The Plant World home page uses square bullets to identify items in the lists and to give the page a more distinctive look. To change the bullet type from the default (disc) to a square or circle, the <ul> tag is entered using the form

```
<ul type="bullettype">
```

where the bullettype value in quotation marks can be disc, square, or circle. If you want to use the default disc bullet, the type attribute does not need to be included.

Table 3-3 on the next page shows the HTML code used to create two unordered (bulleted) lists for the Plant World home page. An h2 heading above each unordered list visually separates the list from other elements on the Web page and indicates what the items in the list describe. The h2 heading tags are used so the list headings are slightly smaller than the main h1 heading.

	Table 3-3 HTML Code for Creating Unordered (Bulleted) Lists	
LINE	**HTML TAG AND TEXT**	
16	<h2>Our company</h2>	
17	<ul type="square">	
18	<li>Founded in 1999 by Jared Adam Smith</li>	
19	<li>Headquartered in Fairfield, Connecticut</li>	
20	<li>38 store locations throughout New England</li>	
21	</ul>	
22		
23	<h2>Our services</h2>	
24	<ul type="square">	
25	<li>Landscape design</li>	
26	<li>Planting and maintenance</li>	
27	<li>Online information for all types of plants</li>	
28	</ul>	

The steps below show how to create the two unordered (bulleted) lists that appear on the Plant World home page.

To Create Unordered (Bulleted) Lists

1

• **If necessary, click line 16.**

2

• **Enter the HTML code shown in Table 3-3.**

3

• **Press the ENTER key twice to insert a blank line on line 29, after the second </ul> in the HTML code.**

The HTML code creates two unordered, or bulleted, lists, with three items each (Figure 3-15). Because the code specifies a type attribute and value of square, the lists will appear in the Web page using a square bullet.

FIGURE 3-15

Adding a Background Image

The Web page created in Project 2 used the bgcolor attribute in the <body> tag to add a background color. The Plant World home page created in this project will use the background attribute of the <body> tag to add the image, greyback.jpg, as the Web page background. Using this image will give the background a grey, lightly textured look.

The following steps show how to add a background image to the Plant World home page. The image file, greyback.jpg, is saved on the HTML Data Disk. See the inside back cover for instructions for downloading the HTML Data Disk, or see your instructor.

To Add a Background Image

1

• **Click immediately to the right of the y in the <body> tag on line 9 and then press the SPACEBAR.**

line 9

2

• **Type** background= "greyback.jpg" **as the attribute.**

The HTML code is displayed (Figure 3-16). The attribute value, greyback.jpg, indicates the file name and location of the image. When the Web page is displayed, it will have a grey, lightly textured background.

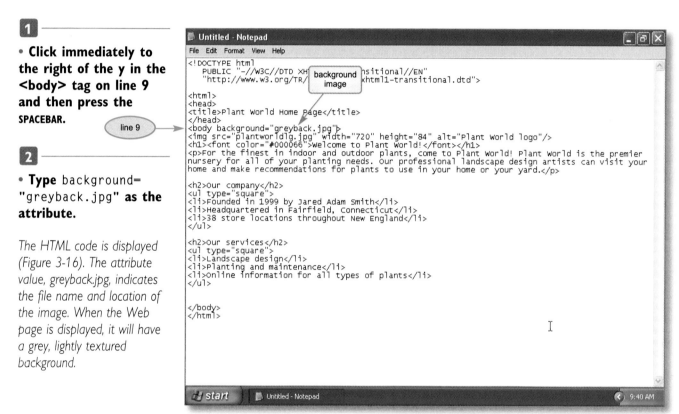

FIGURE 3-16

Adding a Text Link

As you have learned, a Web site is a collection of Web pages created and maintained by a group or individual. Web pages often include links to connect one Web page to another page within the same Web site, so users can move easily from page to page. In this project, the Plant World home page includes a text link to the Desert Plants Web page, which is part of the same Web site.

The <a> and </a> tags are used to create links in a Web page. The <a> tag also is called the anchor tag because it is used to create anchors for links to another page in the same Web site, to a Web page in an external Web site, within the same Web page, and for e-mail links. The basic form of the tag used to create a link is:

```
<a href="URL">linktext</a>
```

where linktext is the clickable word or phrase that appears on the Web page and the value for href (hypertext reference) is the name or URL of the linked page or file. Table 3-4 shows some of the <a> tag attributes and their functions.

Table 3-4 <a> Tag Attributes and Functions	
ATTRIBUTE	FUNCTION
href	Specifies the URL of the linked page or file.
name	Defines a name for the current anchor so it may be the target or destination of another link. Each anchor in a Web page must use a unique name.
rel	Indicates a forward relationship from the current document to the linked document. The value of the rel attribute is a link type, such as prev, next, index, or copyright. For example, the chapter5.htm Web page might include the tag, <a rel="next" href="chapter6.htm"> to indicate a link to the Web page for the next chapter, chapter6.htm.
rev	Indicates a reverse (backward) relationship from the current document to the linked document. The value of the rev attribute is a link type, such as prev, next, index, or copyright. For example, the chapter5.htm Web page might include the tag, <a rel="prev" href="chapter4.htm"> to indicate a link to the Web page for the previous chapter, chapter4.htm.
type	Specifies the content type (also known as media types or MIME types) of the linked page or file to help a browser determine if it can handle the resource type. Examples of content types include text/html, image/jpeg, video/quicktime, application/java, text/css, and text/javascript.

Adding a Text Link to Another Web Page within the Same Web Site

As discussed, the Plant World home page includes a text link to the Desert Plants Web page, which is part of the same Web site. When a visitor clicks the link on the home page, the browser will display the Desert Plants Web page.

Before creating the link, be sure you know the URL or name of the file to be linked and the text that will serve as the clickable word or phrase. The words should be descriptive and tell the Web page visitor the purpose of the link. For the Plant World home page, the text link is a phrase in a paragraph at the bottom of the Web page.

The following steps illustrate how to add a text link to another Web page within the same Web site.

To Add a Text Link to Another Web Page within the Same Web Site

1

• **Click immediately to the right of the </ul> tag on line 28 and then press the DOWN ARROW key twice.**

2

• **With the insertion point on line 30, type** <p>To learn more about the Plant World products and services, please browse the Plant World Web site, where you can find information on all types of plants, both for indoor and outdoor use. You also can learn about this month's featured desert plants, which have a natural beauty that can enhance any landscape!</p> **and then press the ENTER key (Figure 3-17).**

FIGURE 3-17

3

• **Click immediately to the left of the d in desert on line 32.**

• **Type** <a href= "desertplants.htm"> **to start the link.**

• **Click immediately to the right of the s in plants on line 33. Type** </a> **to end the link and then press the ENTER key.**

The HTML code is displayed (Figure 3-18).

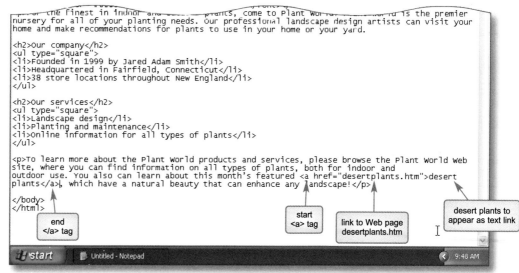

FIGURE 3-18

As shown in Figure 3-17, the <a> and </a> tags enclose the text, desert plants, which will appear on the Plant World home page as a clickable text link. The href attribute value sets the Web page, desertplants.htm, as the linked Web page.

Adding an E-Mail Link

The Plant World home page also includes an e-mail link so customers can contact Plant World for additional information or to comment on the Web page. The <a> and </a> tags used to create a text link to a Web page also are used to create an e-mail link. Instead of using a URL as the href attribute value, the href attribute value for an e-mail link uses the form,

```
<a href="mailto:address@email.com">linktext</a>
```

where the href attribute value uses the word, mailto, to indicate it is an email link, followed by a colon and the e-mail address to which to send the e-mail message. When the browser recognizes a **mailto** URL in a clicked link, it automatically opens a new message in the default e-mail program and inserts the appropriate contact e-mail address in the To field. The clickable text used for an e-mail link typically is the e-mail address used in the e-mail link. The Web page also should provide some information before the link, so visitors know the purpose of the e-mail link.

The following steps show how to add an e-mail link to a Web page.

To Add an E-Mail Link

1

• **With the insertion point on line 34, type** <p>Have a question or comment? Call us at (206) 555-PLANT or e-mail us at plantworld@isp.com. </p> **as a new paragraph of text.**

FIGURE 3-19

2

• **Click immediately before the p in plantworld on line 34. Type** <a href="mailto: plantworld@isp.com"> **to start the e-mail link.**

3

• **Click immediately after the m in com in the e-mail address text. Type** </a> **to end the e-mail link.**

The HTML code for the e-mail link is displayed (Figure 3-19). The HTML code for the Plant World home page is complete.

As shown in Figure 3-19, the <a> and </a> tags enclose the text, plantworld@isp.com, which will appear on the Plant World home page as a clickable e-mail link. The href attribute value, mailto:plantworld@isp.com, indicates that clicking the e-mail link will start a new message addressed to plantworld@isp.com.

Saving and Printing the HTML File

With the HTML code for the Plant World home page complete, the file should be saved and a copy should be printed as a reference.

To Save and Print an HTML File

1 With a floppy disk in drive A, click File on the menu bar and then click Save As. Type plantworld.htm in the File name text box.

2 If necessary, click 3½ Floppy (A:) in the Save in list. Click the Project03 folder and then click the ProjectFiles folder in the list of available folders. Click the Save button in the Save As dialog box.

3 Click File on the menu bar and then click Print on the File menu.

Notepad saves the HTML file in the Project03\ProjectFiles folder on the floppy disk in drive A using the file name, plantworld.htm. Notepad prints the HTML file (Figure 3-20).

```
<!DOCTYPE html
    PUBLIC "-//W3C//DTD XHTML 1.0 Transitional//EN"
    "http://www.w3.org/TR/xhtml1/DTD/xhtml1-transitional.dtd">

<html>
<head>
<title>Plant World Home Page</title>
</head>
<body background="greyback.jpg">
<img src="plantworldlg.jpg" width="720" height="84" alt="Plant World logo"/>
<h1><font color="#000066">Welcome to Plant World!</font></h1>
<p>For the finest in indoor and outdoor plants, come to Plant World! Plant World is
the premier nursery for all of your planting needs. Our professional landscape
design artists can visit your home and make recommendations for plants to use in
your home or your yard.

<h2>Our company</h2>
<ul type="square">
<li>Founded in 1999 by Jared Adam Smith</li>
<li>Headquartered in Fairfield, Connecticut</li>
<li>38 store locations throughout New England</li>
</ul>

<h2>Our services</h2>
<ul type="square">
<li>Landscape design</li>
<li>Planting and maintenance</li>
<li>Online information for all types of plants</li>
</ul>

<p>To learn more about the Plant World products and services, please browse the
Plant World Web site, where you can find information on all types of plants, both
for indoor and
outdoor use. You also can learn about this month's featured <a
href="desertplants.htm">desert plants</a>, which have a natural beauty that can
enhance any landscape!</p>
<p>Have a question or comment? Call us at (206) 555-PLANT or e-mail us at <a
href="mailto:plantworld@isp.com">plantworld@isp.com</a>.</p>

</body>
</html>
```

FIGURE 3-20

Viewing, Testing Links, and Printing a Web Page

After the HTML file for the Plant World home page is saved, it should be viewed in a browser to confirm the Web page appears as desired. It also is important to test the two links in the Plant World home page to verify they function as expected. With the home page displayed in the browser, click the e-mail hyperlink and the desert plants link to verify they work correctly. The second Web page, desertplants.htm, will display, although it is not completed. In the remainder of this project, the HTML code in the desertplants.htm file will be edited to create the Web page shown in Figure 3-1b on page HTM 71.

More About

Web Page Testing

An important part of Web page development is testing Web page links. For more information about link testing, visit the HTML More About Web page (scsite.com/html3e/more.htm) and then click Web Page Testing.

To View a Web Page

1 Click the Start button on the Windows taskbar and then point to All Programs on the Start menu. Click Internet Explorer (or another browser command) on the All Programs submenu.

2 If necessary, click the Maximize button to maximize the browser window.

3 When the browser window appears, click the Address bar.

4 Type a:\Project03\ProjectFiles\plantworld.htm in the Address text box.

5 Press the ENTER key.

Your browser displays the Web page, plantworld.htm (Figure 3-21).

The Plant World home page appears, with the grey textured image as a background and the Plant World logo. The home page uses two different sizes of headings to separate visually the paragraph text and the two unordered lists, which use a square bullet type. Finally, the home page includes a text link to another Web page in the same Web site and an e-mail link.

After confirming that the Web page appears as desired, the two links in the Plant World home page should be tested to verify they function as expected. The following steps show how to test the links in the Plant World home page.

FIGURE 3-21

To Test Links in a Web Page

1

• **Point to the e-mail link, plantworld@isp.com.**

The mouse pointer changes to a pointing hand.

2

• **Click plantworld@isp.com.**

The browser recognizes a mailto URL in the e-mail link and automatically opens a new message in the default e-mail program. A New Message window is displayed (Figure 3-22). The address, plantworld@isp.com, is displayed in the To text box.

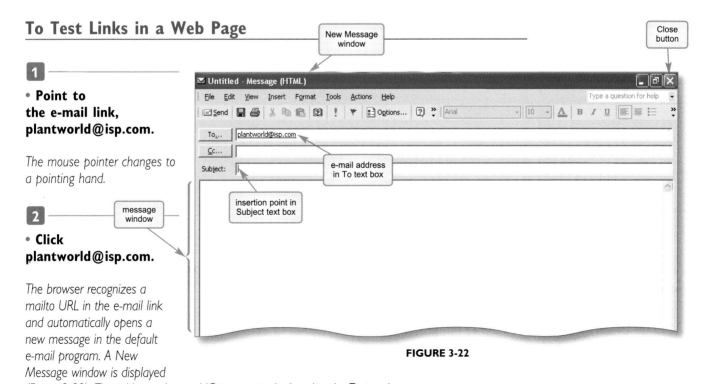

FIGURE 3-22

3

• **Click the Close button in the New Message window.**

4

• **With the HTML Data Disk in drive A, point to the link, desert plants.**

The mouse pointer changes to a pointing hand.

5

• **Click desert plants.**

The desertplants.htm page is displayed (Figure 3-23). This Web page is an HTML document stored in the Project03\ProjectFiles folder on the HTML Data Disk.

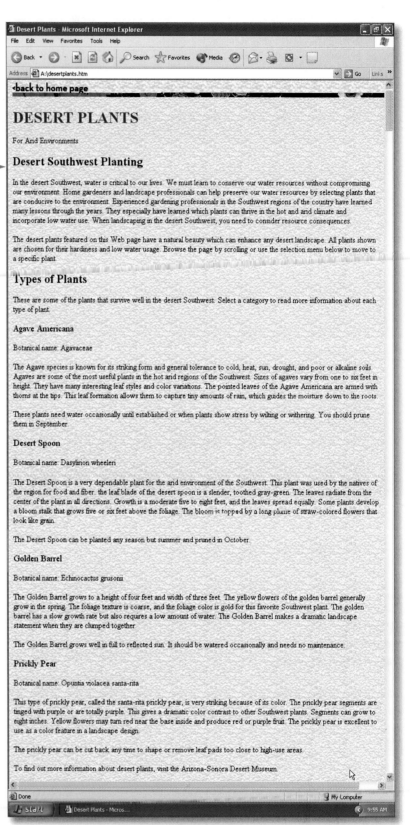

Desert Plants Web page prior to editing

FIGURE 3-23

After verifying that the two links work, scroll through the Web page, desertplants.htm, to view its appearance. The following step shows how to print the Web page for future reference.

To Print a Web Page

1 **Click the Back button on the Standard toolbar to return to the Plant World home page.**

2 **Click the Print button on the Standard toolbar.**

The displayed Web page is printed (Figure 3-24).

FIGURE 3-24

In the following sections, the HTML code in the desertplants.htm file is edited to add images with wrapped text, links within the Desert Plants Web page, a link to another Web site, and an image link back to the home page.

Editing the Second Web Page

The current version of the desertplants.htm Web page is stored on the HTML Data Disk. As shown in Figure 3-23 on page HTM 92, the Desert Plants Web page includes many Web page elements, such as headings, paragraph text, and images.

In this section, you will learn to open the existing Web page file and edit the HTML code so the Desert Plants Web page appears as shown in Figure 3-25. You will learn to enhance the text by adding bold, italics, and color. You also will learn how to add an image and set text to wrap around the image. You also will learn to add three additional types of links: (1) links within the same Web page, (2) a text link to a Web page in another Web site, and (3) and an image link to a Web page in the same Web site.

As you have learned, the <a> tag used to create a link must specify the page, file, or location to which it links. In the case of a link within a Web page, the <a> tag specifies a **target**, or named location, in the same file. Before adding the links and targets in the Desert Plants Web page, an unordered (bulleted) list that contains four items — Agave Americana, Desert Spoon, Golden Barrel, and Prickly Pear — must be added to the page. The list items will serve as the links that are directed to the heading at the top of each major section of the Desert Plants Web page. When clicked, these links will move the Web page visitor to the targets, which are the headings named Agave Americana, Desert Spoon, Golden Barrel, and Prickly Pear, respectively.

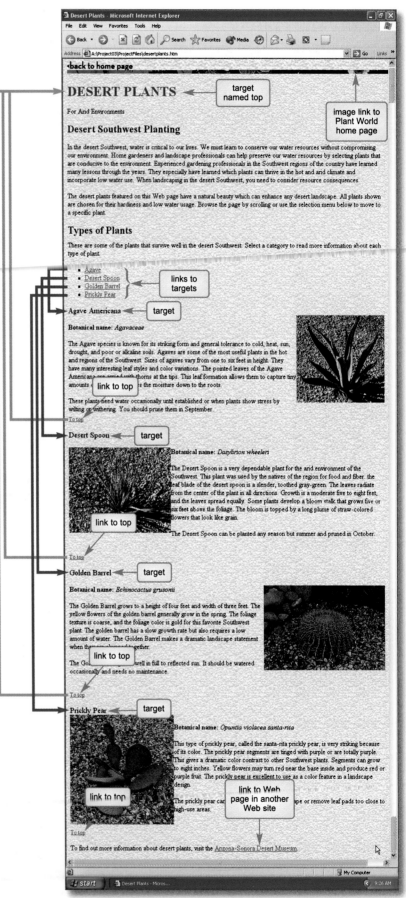

FIGURE 3-25 Completed Desert Plants Web page.

Because the Web page is so long, it is a good design practice to provide users with a quick way to move back to the top of the Web page, without scrolling back. For this purpose, the Web page includes four text links named, To top. These links are located just above the Desert Spoon, Golden Barrel, and Prickly Pear headings, and at the bottom of the page above the link to the Arizona-Sonora Desert Museum. When clicked, the To top link takes the Web page visitor back to the top of the page.

To complete the Desert Plants Web page, an image link will be created, so users can click the back to home page link to return to the Plant World home page. A text link also will be created from the Desert Plants Web page to an external Web site, the Arizona-Sonora Desert Museum.

The following steps illustrate how to open the desertplants.htm file in Notepad.

To Open an HTML File

1 Click the Notepad button on the taskbar.

2 With the HTML Data Disk in drive A, click File on the menu bar and then click Open on the File menu.

3 If necessary, click the Look in box arrow and then click 3½ Floppy (A:). Click the Project03 folder and then click the Project Files folder in the list of available folders.

4 If necessary, click the Files of type box arrow and then click All Files. Click desertplants.htm in the list of files.

5 Click the Open button in the Open dialog box.

The first 39 lines of the HTML code for desertplants.htm are displayed (Figure 3-26).

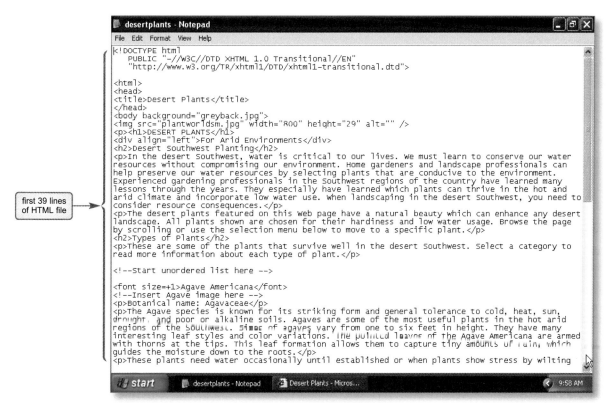

FIGURE 3-26

Formatting Text

Earlier in the project, the color attribute of the <font> tag was used to change the color of text on the Web page. HTML provides a number of other tags to format text, several of which are listed in Table 3-5.

Table 3-5 Text Formatting Tags	
HTML TAG	**FUNCTION**
<b> </b>	Physical style tag that displays text as bold
<big> </big>	Increases the font size in comparison to the surrounding text
<blockquote> </blockquote >	Designates a long quotation; indents margins on sections of text
<em> </em>	Logical style tag that displays text with emphasis (usually appears as italicized)
<i> </i>	Physical style tag that displays text as italicized
<pre> </pre>	Sets enclosed text as preformatted material, meaning it preserves spaces and line breaks; often used for text in column format in another document pasted into HTML code
<small> </small>	Decreases the font size in comparison to the surrounding text
<strong> </strong>	Logical style tag that displays text with strong emphasis (usually appears as bold)
	Displays text as subscript (below normal text)
	Displays text as superscript (above normal text)
<tt> </tt>	Displays text as teletype or monospace text
<u> </u>	Displays text as underlined

Figure 3-27 shows a sample Web page with some of the text format tags. These tags fall into two categories: logical style tags and physical style tags. Logical styles allow a browser to interpret the tag based on browser settings, relative to other text in a Web page. The <h2> heading tag, for example, is a logical style that indicates that the heading text should be larger than regular text but smaller than text formatted using an <h1> heading tag. The <strong> </strong> tag is another logical style, which indicates that text should have a strong emphasis, and which most browsers interpret as displaying the text in bold font. Physical style tags specify a particular font change that is interpreted strictly by all browsers. For example, to ensure that text appears as bold font, you would enclose it between a start <b> and end </b> tag. In practice, the <strong> and <b> tags usually have the same result when the Web page displays.

Changing the characteristics of text can help call attention to that portion of text. You should use these elements with discretion, however. A Web page with too much bold, italicized, or other types of formatted text can be difficult to read.

More About

Text Formatting

You can indent entire blocks of text by using the <blockquote> </blockquote> tags. Both Internet Explorer and Netscape Communicator indent the text on either side by 40 pixels. You can use <p> and <br /> tags within the blockquote tags to control line breaking within the text.

Formatting Text In Bold

Figure 3-25 on page HTM 94 shows the final version of the Desert Plants Web page. As shown in the figure, bold text is used for the phrase, Botanical Name:, which appears once for each of the four plant types listed. The following steps illustrate how to format text in bold.

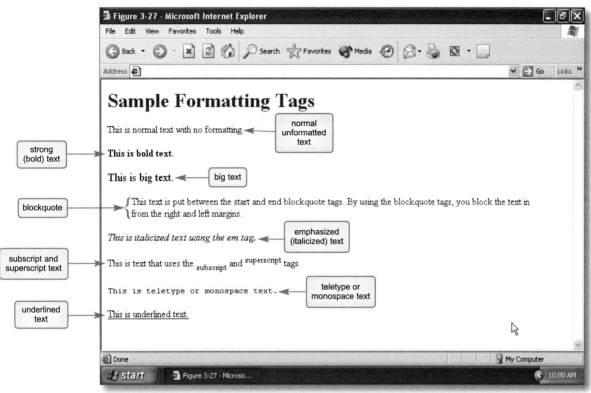

FIGURE 3-27 Examples of various text formatting tags.

To Format Text in Bold

1

• Click immediately to the left of the B in Botanical on line 32. Type `<b>` as the start tag (Figure 3-28).

2

• Click immediately to the right of the colon (:) in Botanical name: on line 32 and then type `</b>` as the end tag.

FIGURE 3-28

3

• **Repeat Steps 1 and 2 to bold the other three occurrences of the phrase, Botanical name:, on lines 45, 57, and 69.**

The bold tags surround the words, Botanical name:, on line 32, 45, 57, and 69 (Figure 3-29).

line 32

line 45

line 57

line 69

FIGURE 3-29

Formatting Text in Italics

As shown in Figure 3-25 on page HTM 94, the botanical names for each type of plant appear in italics. The following steps show how to use the <em> tag to italicize the botanical names for each type of plant.

To Format Text in Italics

1

• **Click immediately to the right of the </b> on line 32. Type** `<em>` **as the start tag.**

2

• **Click immediately to the right of the e at the end of Agavaceae on line 32. Type** `</em>` **as the end tag.**

3

• **Repeat Steps 1 and 2 to italicize the other botanical names on lines 45, 57, and 69.**

The tags, <em> and </em>, surround the botanical names Agavaceae, Dasylirion wheeleri, Echinocactus grusonii, and Opuntia violacea santa-rita on lines 32, 45, 57, and 69 (Figure 3-30).

line 32

line 45

line 57

line 69

begin em tag

end em tag

FIGURE 3-30

Format Text with a Font Color

Changing the color of the text also can enhance its look. As shown in Figure 3-25 on page HTM 94, the main heading, DESERT PLANTS, displays in dark blue. The following steps show how to use the color attribute of the <font> tag to format a heading in color.

More About

HTML Colors

Color is an important aspect of Web development. Visually appealing Web sites attract visitors. For more information about HTML color, visit the HTML More About Web page (scsite.com/html3e/more.htm) and then click Coloring Web Graphics.

To Format Text with a Font Color

1

• **Click immediately to the left of the word, DESERT, on line 11. Type** `<font color="#000099">` **as the start tag.**

2

• **Click immediately to the right of the word, PLANTS, on line 11. Type** `</font>` **as the end tag.**

The HTML code used to format the heading is displayed (Figure 3-31). The color attribute uses a six-digit number code of #000099 to specify that the heading should appear in a dark blue color.

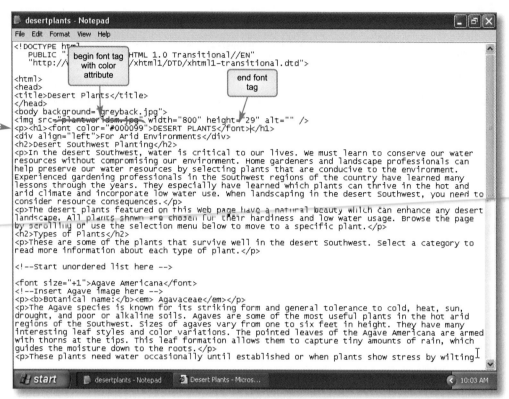

FIGURE 3-31

Adding an Image with Wrapped Text

As shown in Table 2-3 on page HTM 52, the <img> tag has many attributes, including attributes to specify height, width, alignment, alternate text, and so on. In Project 2, the HTML code used the height and width attributes to identify the size of the image to the browser and the alt attribute to define the text that displays when the user moves the mouse over the image.

Alignment also is a key consideration when inserting an image. Alignment can give an image and the surrounding text completely different looks. Figure 3-32 shows an image that is right-aligned, which wraps any text to the left of the image. The format of the HTML code to add the right-aligned image is

```
<img src="agave.jpg" align="right" alt= "Agave" width="212"
height="203" />.
```

where the src attribute indicates the file name of the image file, align="right" aligns the image to the right of the text, the height and width are in number of pixels, and the alt attribute displays the alternate text as the image is loading. The text used in the alt attribute helps to keep the visitor informed of what is going to display when the image has loaded completely.

The completed Desert Plants Web page, as shown in Figure 3-25 on page HTM 94, uses both right-aligned and left-aligned images. After specifying an image alignment and defining how text wraps, you also must enter a break (<br />) tag to stop the text wrapping. To end right-aligned text wrap, enter the <br clear="right" /> tag where the text should stop wrapping to the right. Figure 3-33 shows a left-aligned image, with text wrapped to its left. In the left-aligned example, the <br clear="left" /> tag is used to end the text wrap. The <br clear="all" /> tag clears both left and right alignments.

In addition to aligning text to the right and left of an image, the align attribute also supports values to align text with the top, middle, or bottom of the image, vertically. Figure 3-34a on the next page shows an example of one line of text with align="top" used in the <img> tag. This aligns the tagged text with the top of the image, with the remainder of the text displaying below the image. Figure 3-34b shows the same text with the align="middle" attribute, and Figure 3-34c on the following page shows the same text with the align="bottom" attribute.

FIGURE 3-32 Right-aligned image.

FIGURE 3-33 Left-aligned image.

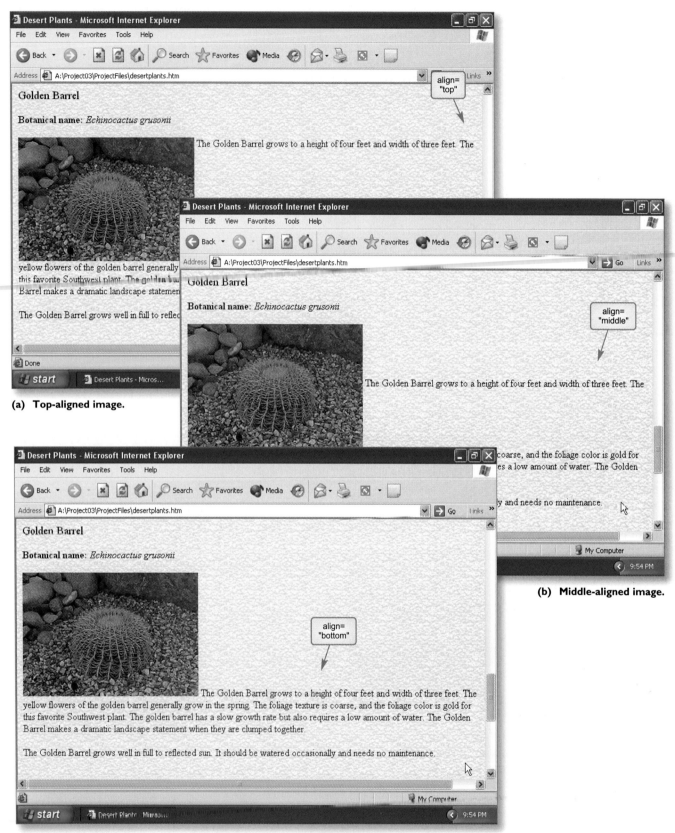

(a) Top-aligned image.

(b) Middle-aligned image.

(c) Bottom-aligned image.

FIGURE 3-34

Adding an Image with Wrapped Text

The following steps show how to insert right-aligned images with wrapped text, as shown in Figure 3-32 on page HTM 101. The images are saved on the HTML Data Disk in the Project03\ProjectFiles folder. See the inside back cover for instructions for downloading the HTML Data Disk, or see your instructor.

To Add an Image with Wrapped Text

1

• **Highlight the words `<!--Insert Agave image here -->` on line 31.**

2

• **Type `<img src="agave.jpg" align="right" alt= "Agave" width="212" height="203" />` and do not press the ENTER key.**

The HTML code inserts an image with the file name, agave.jpg (Figure 3-35). The image will be right-aligned on the Web page, with text wrapped to its left.

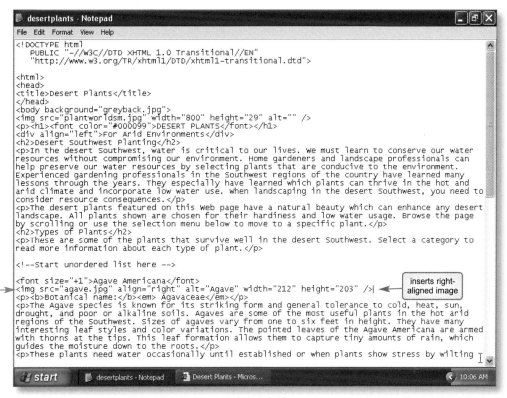

FIGURE 3-35

3

• **Highlight the words `<!--Insert Desert Spoon image here -->` on line 44.**

4

• **Type `<img src="desertspoon.jpg" align="left" alt= "Desert Spoon" width="245" height="198" />` to insert a left-aligned image with wrapped text.**

5

• **Highlight the words `<!--Insert Golden Barrel image here -->` on line 56.**

6

• **Type `<img src="goldenbarrel.jpg" align="right" alt= "Golden Barrel" width="292" height="197" />` to insert a right-aligned image with wrapped text.**

7

• **Highlight the words <!-- Insert Prickly Pear image here --> on line 68.** *(line 31)*

8

• **Type <img src= "pricklypear.jpg" align="left" alt= "Prickly Pear" width="250" height="255" /> to insert a left-aligned image with wrapped text.** *(line 44)* *(line 56)*

The HTML code for all four images appears, as shown in Figure 3-36. *(line 68)*

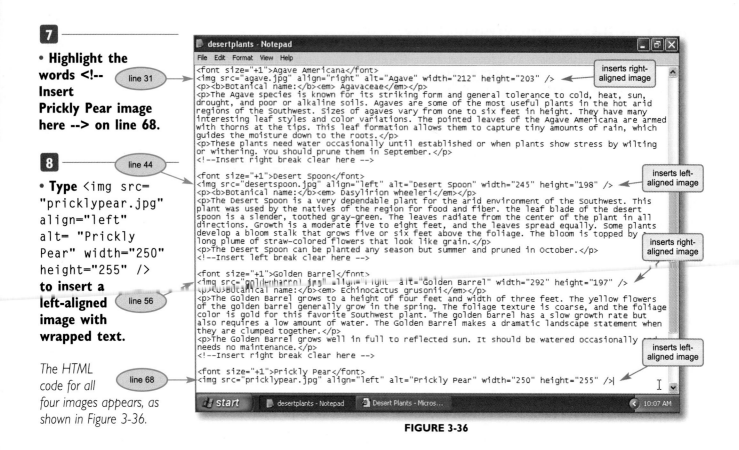

FIGURE 3-36

The HTML code entered in the previous steps sets the images to alternate alignment (first right, then left, then right, then left) down the Desert Plants Web page to provide a visually appealing and balanced Web page.

Clearing the Text Wrapping

The steps above illustrate how to insert an image and wrap the text to the right or the left. Next, the break tags to clear the text wrapping must be entered, using the <br clear=" " /> tag, with right, left, or all as the clear attribute value in the quotation marks. The following steps show to enter code to clear the text wrapping.

To Clear the Text Wrapping

1

• **Highlight the words <!--Insert right break clear here --> on line 41 and then type <br clear="right" /> as the tag.**

2

• **Highlight the words `<!--Insert right break clear here -->` on line 65 and then type** `<br clear="right" />` **as the tag.**

The HTML code to clear the text wrapping for both right-aligned images is displayed (Figure 3-37).

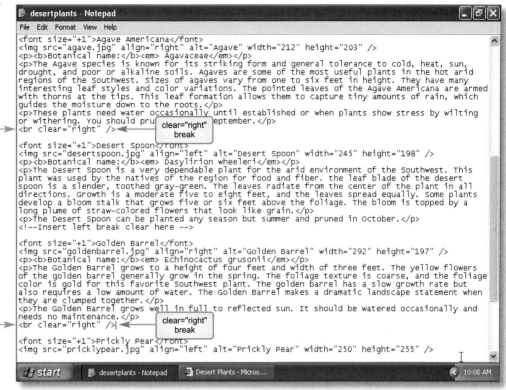

FIGURE 3-37

3

• **Highlight the words `<!--Insert left break clear here -->` on line 53 and then type** `<br clear="left" />` **as the tag.**

4

• **Highlight the words `<!--Insert left break clear here -->` on line 77 and then type** `<br clear="left" />` **as the tag.**

The HTML code to clear the text wrapping for both left-aligned images is displayed (Figure 3-38). The text wrapping breaks all are in place on lines 41, 53, 65, and 77.

FIGURE 3-38

The previous steps used several image attributes when adding images, including the alignment, the height and width, and the alternate text. The <img> tag also supports additional attributes to control the spacing around images and text.

More About

Web Page Size

The size of a Web page is the total file size of all elements, including the HTML file and any images. The more images a Web page contains, the longer it takes to download. When adding images, test the download time; if it takes more than 10 seconds, most users will not wait to view the page.

Using Horizontal and Vertical Spacing

Using spacing between and around images and text can help create an easy-to-read Web page, as shown in Figure 3-39. The hspace and vspace attributes of the <img> tag control the amount of horizontal and vertical space around an image. If text is wrapped around an image, as it is on the Desert Plants Web page, adding space around the image helps ensure that the text does not appear to run into the image. Figure 3-39 shows images added to a Web page using hspace and vspace attributes. Additional vertical space displays above and below the image where the <img> tag uses the attribute and value, vspace="20". Additional horizontal space displays to the right and the left of the image where the <img> tag uses the attribute and value, hspace="20".

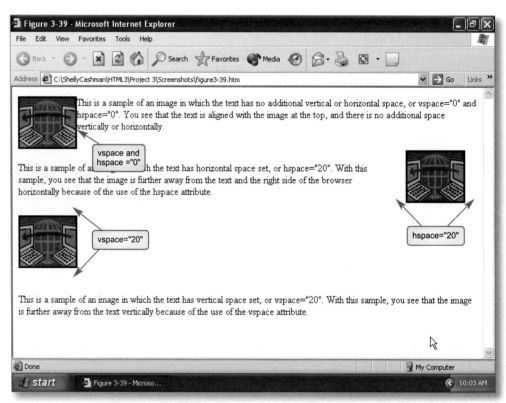

FIGURE 3-39 Examples of horizontal and vertical spacing.

Using Thumbnail Images

Many Web developers use thumbnail images to improve page loading time. A **thumbnail image** is a smaller version of the image itself. The thumbnail is used as a link that, when clicked, will load the full-sized image. Figure 3-40a shows an example of a thumbnail image. When the image is clicked, the browser loads the full-sized image (Figure 3-40b). Loading images can take a long time, depending on the size and the complexity of the image. Using a thumbnail image gives a visitor the opportunity to decide whether to view the full-sized image.

(a) Thumbnail image.

(b) Full-sized

FIGURE 3-40

To create a thumbnail version of an image, the image can be resized to a smaller size in a paint or image-editing project and then saved with a different file name. The thumbnail image then is added to a Web page as an image link to the larger version of the image. The HTML code to add a thumbnail image that links to a larger image takes the form

```
<a href="largeimage.gif"><img src="thumbnail.gif" /></a>
```

where largeimage.gif is the name of the full-sized image and thumbnail.gif is the name of the smaller version of the image. If a visitor clicks the thumbnail image to view the larger image, he or she can use the Back button on the browser's Standard toolbar to return to the original Web page displaying the thumbnail image.

Obtaining Images

You can obtain images from a number of different sources. The Web contains many Web sites with thousands of image files on countless subjects that can be downloaded free and used for noncommercial purposes. Using a search engine, enter a search for the phrases, free GIFs or free Web images, to find collections of images for use on a Web site. If you find a graphic you want to use, right-click the image, click Save Picture As on the shortcut menu, and then save the image to your computer.

Many applications come with clip art that can be used on Web pages. Other types of digital images, such as images scanned by a scanner or pictures taken with a digital camera, also can be included on a Web page. You also can create images using a paint or image-editing program. Regardless of where you get the images, always be aware of copyright rules and regulations.

More About

E-mail Links

Although it is not common, you can assign more than one e-mail address to a mailto: tag. Use the form "mailto:first@isp.com, second@isp.com" in the <a href=> tag. Some older browsers may not support this tag.

Adding a Text Link to Another Web Site

As you have learned, one of the more important features of the Web is the capability of linking a Web page in one Web site to a Web page in another Web site anywhere in the world. The <a> and </a> tags used to create a text link to a Web page within the same Web site also are used to create a link to a Web page in another Web site.

Adding a Text Link to a Web Page in Another Web Site

In this project, the Desert Plants Web page includes a link to a Web page on another Web site, where the visitor can find additional desert plant information. The <a> and </a> tags are used to create a link to a Web page in another Web site. The basic form of the tag used to create a link is the same as the previous links. To link to a Web page on an external Web site, the href (hypertext reference) attribute value includes the entire URL to the Web page (for example, http://www.desertmuseum.org). The phrase, Arizona-Sonora Desert Museum, is used as the clickable text link.

The following steps illustrate how to add a text link on the Desert Plants Web page to the home page of the Arizona-Sonora Desert Museum Web site.

To Add a Text Link to a Web Page in Another Web Site

1

• **Click immediately to the left of Arizona on line 80 and type** <a href="http://www .desertmuseum.org"> **to add the text link.**

2

• **Click immediately to the right of Museum on line 81 and type** </a> **to end the tag.**

The HTML code is displayed (Figure 3-41).

FIGURE 3-41

After adding this link, the Web page displays as shown in Figure 3-42. The text link displays in a blue, underlined font to indicate it is a link. The mouse pointer also changes to the pointing hand when moved over the link text.

FIGURE 3-42 Web page with external link.

Adding Links within a Web Page

The final links to be added in this project are links within the Desert Plants Web page. Because the Desert Plants is a long page, it would be easier for the visitors to have a menu or list at the top of the Web page that facilitates immediate movement to another section. The Web page in Figure 3-25 on page HTM 94 shows how these links will appear when completed.

Figure 3-43a on the next page shows how clicking the text link, Agave Americana, at the top of the page, links to the Agave Americana section in another part of the Web page (Figure 3-43b). When the mouse pointer is moved over the word, Agave Americana, and clicked, the browser repositions, or links, the page to the target named Agave Americana.

To create links within the same Web page, the targets for the links first must be created. A **target** is a named location or anchor within a Web page to which a link can be created. In the Desert Plants Web page, the internal links are intended to make it easier for Web page visitors to go quickly from the top of the Desert Plants Web page to the Agave Americana, Desert Spoon, Golden Barrel, and Prickly Pear sections of the Web page. Targets thus must be set at the beginning of these four sections, so links then can be created to these targets. To do this, you create a list of words to use as links. The unordered (bulleted) list shown in Figure 3-25 is used as the series of links to the targets.

More About

Other Links

You also can create a link to other Web pages (i.e., non-http), an FTP site, and newsgroups. To link to an FTP site, type `ftp://URL` rather than `http://URL` used in this project. For a newsgroup, type `news:newsgroup` name and for any particular article within the newsgroup, type `news:article` name as the entry.

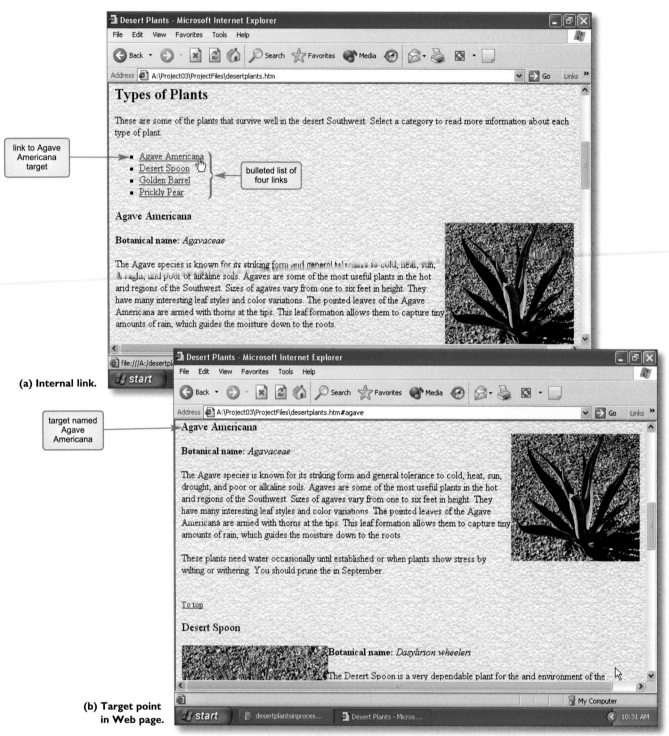

FIGURE 3-43

Setting Link Targets

Link targets are created using the <a> tag with the name attribute, using the form

```
<a name= "targetname"></a>
```

where targetname is a unique name for a link target within that Web page. Notice that the tag uses the name attribute, rather than the href attribute, and that no text is included between the start <a> and end </a> tag, because the target is not intended to display on the Web page as a clickable link. Instead, the link target is intended to mark a specific area of the Web page, to which a link can be directed. The following steps show how to set the four link targets in the Desert Plants Web page.

To Set Link Targets

1

- **Click immediately to the left of the <font> tag on line 30.**

- **Type** <a name= "agaveamericana"></a> **to create a link target named agaveamericana.**

2

- **Click immediately to the left of the <font> tag on line 43.**

- **Type** <a name= "desertspoon"></a> **to create a link target named desertspoon.**

The HTML code is displayed (Figure 3-44). Two link targets, agaveamericana and desertspoon, are created in the Web page.

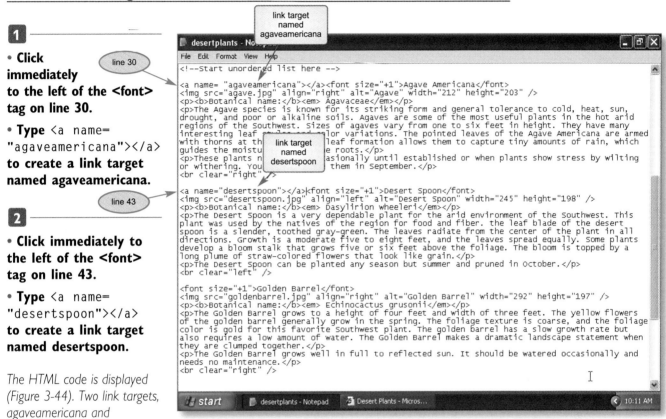

FIGURE 3-44

3

• **Click immediately to the left of the <font> tag on line 55.**

• **Type** <a name= "goldenbarrel"></a> **to create a link target named goldenbarrel.**

4

• **Click immediately to the left of the <font> tag on line 67.**

• **Type** <a name= "pricklypear"></a> **to create a link target named pricklypear.**

The HTML code is displayed (Figure 3-45). Two additional link targets, goldenbarrel and pricklypear, are created in the Web page.

FIGURE 3-45

The four link targets (agaveamericana, desertspoon, goldenbarrel, and pricklypear) now are added to the Desert Plants Web page. With the link targets added, links directed at those tags can be created.

Adding Links to Link Targets within a Web Page

Links to link targets are created using the <a> tag with the name attribute, using the form

```
<a href="#targetname">
```

where targetname is the name of a link target in that Web page. Notice that the tag uses the href attribute, followed by the pound sign (#) and the target name enclosed in quotation marks. The steps on the next page illustrate how to create an unordered (bulleted) list and then to use the list items as links to link targets within the Web page.

To Add Links to Link Targets within a Web Page

1

• **Highlight the words `<!--Start unordered list here -->` on line 28.**

2

• **Type `<ul type="square">` and then press the ENTER key.**

3

• **Type `<li><a href= "#agaveamericana"> Agave Americana </a></li>` and then press the ENTER key.**

The HTML code is displayed (Figure 3-46). The first list item, which displays as a text link, links to the target named agaveamericana.

FIGURE 3-46

4

• **Type `<li><a href="#desertspoon"> Desert Spoon</a></li>` and then press the ENTER key.**

5

• **Type `<li><a href= "#goldenbarrel"> Golden Barrel</a> </li>` and then press the ENTER key.**

6

• **Type `<li><a href= "#pricklypear"> Prickly Pear</a> </li>` and then press the ENTER key.**

• **Type `</ul>` and then press the ENTER key.**

FIGURE 3-47

The HTML code is displayed (Figure 3-47).

More About

Specifying Alternative Fonts

If a Web page font is not available on users' computers, you can create a list of fonts and the browser will determine the font to use. For example, if the Web page uses a Geneva font, but would display well in Arial or Helvetica, you create a comma-separated list of acceptable fonts, using <font face="geneva,arial,helvetica">your text</font> as the code.

The HTML code added to the Desert Plants Web page creates a list with four items. Each item in the list is a text link to a specific, named link target in the Desert Plants Web page.

Adding Links to a Link Target at the Top of the Page

As discussed, it is good design practice to provide users with a quick way to move back to the top of a long Web page. The Desert Plants Web page thus includes four text links named To top, as shown in Figure 3-25 on page HTM 94. Clicking a To top link quickly moves the visitor back to the top of the page. To create these links, first you need to set the target at the top of the page. Then you create four links to that target after the Agave Americana, Desert Spoon, Golden Barrel, and Prickly Pear sections. The links will use a font size smaller than normal text (<font size="-1">), so they do not clutter the Web page. The following steps illustrate how to add links to a target at the top of the page.

To Add Links to a Target at the Top of the Page

1

• **Click to the left of the < symbol on line 10 and then press the ENTER key.**

2

line 10

• **Position the insertion point on line 10 and type** <a name="top"></a> **as the tag.**

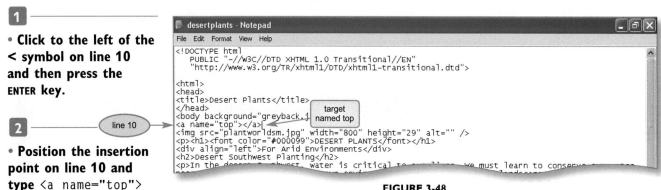

FIGURE 3-48

The target is set at the top of the Web page (Figure 3-48).

3

• **Position the insertion point on the blank line 48 and then type** <p><a href="#top"><font size=-1>To top</font></a></p> **as the tag.**

4

line 48

• **Press the ENTER key.**

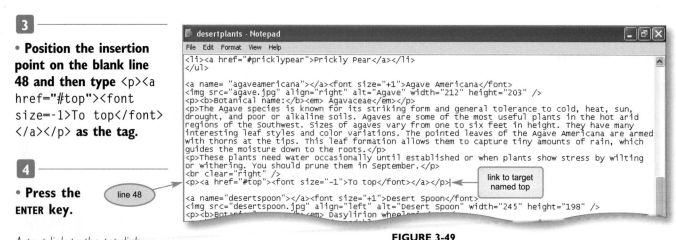

FIGURE 3-49

A text link to the top link target is added (Figure 3-49). The font size is set to -1, so the text link appears smaller than normal text.

After the code for one of the To top links is added, that code can be copied and pasted into other areas of the HTML code. Copying and pasting the code typically is much faster than retyping the code and is less prone to typing errors. The following steps show how to copy and paste the link code to three other lines in the HTML code.

To Copy and Paste HTML Code

1

- **Highlight the HTML code, `<p><a href= "#top"><font size= -1> To top </font> </a></p>`, on line 48.** *(line 61)*
- **Click Edit on the menu bar and then click Copy.**

2

- **Position the insertion point on line 61.** *(line 74)*
- **Click Edit on the menu bar and then click Paste.**
- **Press the ENTER key.** *(line 88)*

3

- **Repeat Step 2 to paste the HTML code on lines 74 and 88.**

The HTML code is displayed (Figure 3-50).

FIGURE 3-50

The HTML code added to lines 48, 61, 74, and 88 creates four text links that are directed to the link target named, top, at the top of the Desert Plants Web page. For each text link, the HTML code creates a new paragraph using the `<p>` and `</p>` tags, sets the font to a small size using the `<font size="-1">` and the `</font>` tags, and sets the link to the top target `<a href="#top"></a>` using the anchor tag.

Adding an Image Link to a Web Page

The last step in editing the Desert Plants Web page is to add an image link from the Desert Plants Web page back to the Plant World home page. The steps on the next page show how to create an image link at the top of the Desert Plants Web page that a visitor can click to return to the Plant World home page.

To Add an Image Link to a Web Page

1

• **Click immediately to the left of <img on line 11.**

• **Type** `<a href= "plantworld.htm">` **as the tag and** *(line 11)* **then press the ENTER key.**

2

• **Click immediately to the right of alt=" " /> on line 12.**

• **Type** `</a>` **as the tag.**

The HTML file is displayed (Figure 3-51). The image, plantworldsm.jpg is set as an image link to plantworld.htm.

FIGURE 3-51

3

• **Click immediately to the left of alt=" " /> on line 12.**

• **Type** `border="0"` **and then press the SPACEBAR.**

The HTML file is displayed (Figure 3-52).

FIGURE 3-52

The image, plantworldsm.jpg, is added to the top of the Desert Plants Web page. The <a> </a> tags are used to set the image as the clickable element for the link, which connects to the home page, plantworld.htm. Setting the image border attribute value to zero ensures that no border displays around the image. As previously discussed, if the image did have a border, the border would display using the default link colors to indicate that the link is normal, active, or visited. Because it does not have a border, no link colors display.

Saving and Printing the HTML File and Web Page

With the HTML code for the Desert Plants Web page complete, the HTML file should be saved and a copy should be printed as a reference.

To Save and Print the HTML File

1 **Save the HTML file by clicking File on the menu bar and then clicking Save on the File menu.**

2 **Click File on the menu bar and then click Print on the File menu.**

Notepad prints the HTML file (Figure 3-53). Notepad saves the HTML file in the Project03\ ProjectFiles folder on the floppy disk in drive A using the file name, desertplants.htm.

FIGURE 3-53

```
<p><b>Botanical name:</b> <em>Echinocactus grusonii</em></p>
<p>The Golden Barrel grows to a height of four feet and width of three feet. The yellow
flowers of the golden barrel generally grow in the spring. The foliage texture is coarse, and
the foliage color is gold for this favorite Southwest plant. The golden barrel has a slow
growth rate but also requires a low amount of water. The Golden Barrel makes a dramatic
landscape statement when they are clumped together.</p>
<p>The Golden Barrel grows well in full to reflected sun. It should be watered occasionally
and needs no maintenance.</p>
<br clear="right" />
<p><a href="#top"><font size=-1>To top</font></a></p>

<a name="pricklypear"></a><font size=+1>Prickly Pear</font>
<img src="pricklypear.jpg" align="left" alt= "Prickly Pear" width="250" height="255" />
<p><b>Botanical name:</b> <em>Opuntia violacea santa-rita</em></p>
<p>This type of prickly pear, called the santa-rita prickly pear, is very striking because of
its color. The prickly pear segments are tinged with purple or are totally purple. This gives
a dramatic color contrast to other Southwest plants. Segments can grow to eight inches. Yellow
flowers may turn red near the base inside and produce red or purple fruit. The prickly pear is
excellent to use as a color feature in a landscape design.</p>
<p>The prickly pear can be cut back any time to shape or remove leaf pads too close to
high-use areas.</p>
<br clear="left" />
<p><a href="#top"><font size=-1>To top</font></a></p>

<p>To find out more information about desert plants, visit the <a
href="http://www.desertmuseum.org">Arizona-Sonora Desert Museum</a>.</p>
</body>
</html>
```

- 2 -

FIGURE 3-53 (continued)

After the HTML file for the Desert Plants Web page is saved, it should be viewed in a browser to confirm that the Web page appears as desired. It also is important to test the links in the Desert Plants Web page to verify they function as expected. Finally, a copy of the Web page should be printed as a reference.

To View and Test a Web Page

1 **Click the Desert Plants button on the taskbar.**

2 **Click the Refresh button on the Standard toolbar.**

The edited Desert Plants Web page is displayed, as shown in Figure 3-25 on page HTM 94.

With the home page displayed in the browser, click each of the links in the page to verify each link connects to the appropriate Web page or link target. If possible, view the Web page in more than one browser type or version (for example, Microsoft Internet Explorer and Netscape Navigator) to ensure that the Web pages display correctly in different browsers. After testing the links, the Web page can be printed for future reference.

More About

Logical vs. Physical Styles

For more information about the differences between logical and physical styles, visit the HTML More About Web page (scsite.com/html3e/more.htm) and then click Logical vs. Physical Styles.

To Print a Web Page

1 **Click the Print button on the Standard toolbar.**

The Web page prints (Figure 3-54).

Both Web pages in the Plant World Web site are complete. The following steps show how to quit Notepad and a browser.

FIGURE 3-54

To Quit Notepad and a Browser

1 **Click the Close button on the browser title bar.**

2 **Click the Close button on the Notepad window title bar.**

Both the browser and Notepad windows close, and the Windows desktop is displayed.

Project Summary

In this project, you learned how to develop a two-page Web site by creating a home page for Plant World and editing the Desert Plants Web page. You learned the terms and definitions related to linking, as well as how to create a text or link image to a Web page in the same Web site, how to create a text link to a Web page in another Web site, how to create links within the same Web page, and how to create an e-mail link. You also learned to format fonts using bold, italics, and colors. Finally, the project presented more about Web page images, including how to add a background image and how to add an image with wrapped text using various alignments.

What You Should Know

Having completed this project, you should be able to perform the tasks listed below. The tasks are listed in the same order they were presented in this project.

1. Start Notepad (HTM 72)
2. Enter HTML Tags to Define the Web Page Structure (HTM 79)
3. Add an Image (HTM 80)
4. Add a Left-Aligned Heading with a Font Color (HTM 82)
5. Enter a Paragraph of Text (HTM 83)
6. Create Unordered (Bulleted) Lists (HTM 84)
7. Add a Background Image (HTM 85)
8. Add a Text Link to Another Web Page within the Same Web Site (HTM 86)
9. Add an E-Mail Link (HTM 88)
10. Save and Print an HTML File (HTM 89)
11. View a Web Page (HTM 90)
12. Test Links in a Web Page (HTM 91)
13. Print a Web Page (HTM 93)
14. Open an HTML File (HTM 95)
15. Format Text in Bold (HTM 97)
16. Format Text in Italics (HTM 98)
17. Format Text with a Font Color (HTM 99)
18. Add an Image with Wrapped Text (HTM 103)
19. Clear the Text Wrapping (HTM 104)
20. Add a Text Link to a Web Page in Another Web Site (HTM 108)
21. Set Link Targets (HTM 111)
22. Add Links to Link Targets within a Web Page (HTM 113)
23. Add Links to a Target at the Top of the Page (HTM 114)
24. Copy and Paste HTML Code (HTM 115)
25. Add an Image Link to a Web Page (HTM 116)
26. Save and Print the HTML File (HTM 117)
27. View and Test a Web Page (HTM 118)
28. Print a Web Page (HTM 119)
29. Quit Notepad and a Browser (HTM 119)

Learn It Online

Instructions: To complete the Learn It Online exercises, start your browser, click the Address bar, and then enter the Web address `scsite.com/html3e/learn`. When the HTML Learn It Online page is displayed, follow the instructions in the exercises below. Each exercise has instructions for printing your results, either for your own records or for submission to your instructor.

1 Project Reinforcement TF, MC, and SA

Below HTML Project 3, click the Project Reinforcement link. Print the quiz by clicking Print on the File menu for each page. Answer each question.

2 Flash Cards

Below HTML Project 3, click the Flash Cards link and read the instructions. Type 20 (or a number specified by your instructor) in the Number of playing cards text box, type your name in the Enter your Name text box, and then click the Flip Card button. When the flash card is displayed, read the question and then click the ANSWER box arrow to select an answer. Flip through Flash Cards. If your score is 15 (75%) correct or greater, click Print on the File menu to print your results. If your score is less than 15 (75%) correct, then redo this exercise by clicking the Replay button.

3 Practice Test

Below HTML Project 3, click the Practice Test link. Answer each question, enter your first and last name at the bottom of the page, and then click the Grade Test button. When the graded practice test is displayed on your screen, click Print on the File menu to print a hard copy. Continue to take practice tests until you score 80% or better.

4 Who Wants To Be a Computer Genius?

Below HTML Project 3, click the Computer Genius link. Read the instructions, enter your first and last name at the bottom of the page, and then click the PLAY button. When your score is displayed, click the PRINT RESULTS link to print a hard copy.

5 Wheel of Terms

Below HTML Project 3, click the Wheel of Terms link. Read the instructions, and then enter your first and last name and your school name. Click the PLAY button. When your score is displayed, right-click the score and then click Print on the shortcut menu to print a hard copy.

6 Crossword Puzzle Challenge

Below HTML Project 3, click the Crossword Puzzle Challenge link. Read the instructions, and then enter your first and last name. Click the SUBMIT button. Work the crossword puzzle. When you are finished, click the Submit button. When the crossword puzzle is redisplayed, click the Print Puzzle button to print a hard copy.

7 Tips and Tricks

Below HTML Project 3, click the Tips and Tricks link. Click a topic that pertains to Project 3. Right-click the information and then click Print on the shortcut menu. Construct a brief example of what the information relates to in HTML to confirm you understand how to use the tip or trick.

8 Newsgroups

Below HTML Project 3, click the Newsgroups link. Click a topic that pertains to Project 3. Print three comments.

9 Expanding Your Horizons

Below HTML Project 3, click the Expanding Your Horizons link. Click a topic that pertains to Project 3. Print the information. Construct a brief example of what the information relates to in HTML to confirm you understand the contents of the article.

10 Search Sleuth

Below HTML Project 3, click the Search Sleuth link. To search for a term that pertains to this project, select a term below the Project 3 title and then use the Google search engine at google.com (or any major search engine) to display and print two Web pages that present information on the term.

11 Online Help I

Below HTML Project 3, click the Online Help I link. Follow the instructions on the page to access Web pages that provide additional help on project topics. Hand in any printed information to your instructor.

12 Online Help II

Below HTML Project 3, click the Online Help II link. Follow the instructions on the page to access Web pages that provide additional help on project topics. Hand in any printed information to your instructor.

Apply Your Knowledge

1 Editing the Apply Your Knowledge Web Page

Instructions: Start Notepad. Open the file, apply3-1.htm, from the Project03\AYK folder on the HTML Data Disk. If you do not have the HTML Data Disk, see the inside back cover for instructions or see your instructor. The apply3-1.htm file is a partially completed HTML file that contains some errors. Figure 3-55 shows the Apply Your Knowledge Web page as it should display in your browser after the errors are corrected. Perform the following steps using a computer:

1. Enter the URL, `a:\Project03\AYK\apply3-1.htm`, to view the Web page in your browser.
2. Examine the HTML file in Notepad and its appearance as a Web page in the browser.
3. Correct the HTML errors, making the Web page look similar to the one shown in Figure 3-55, with all links working correctly. (*Hint*: review the hspace attribute of the <img> tag.)

FIGURE 3-55

Apply Your Knowledge

4. Add any HTML code necessary for additional features shown in the Web page.

5. Save the revised file in the Project03\AYK folder using the file name, apply3-1solution.htm.

6. Print the revised HTML file.

7. Enter the URL, `a:\Project03\AYK\apply3-1solution.htm`, to view the Web page in your browser.

8. Print the Web page.

9. Write your name on both printouts and hand them in to your instructor.

In the Lab

1 Creating a Web Page with Target Links

Problem: Your instructor wants you to create a Web page demonstrating your knowledge of link targets. You have been asked to create a Web page to demonstrate this technique, similar to the one shown in Figure 3-56.

FIGURE 3-56

Instructions: Start Notepad. Perform the following steps using a computer:

1. Start a new HTML file with the title, Lab 3-1 [your name], in the main heading section.
2. Begin the body section by adding the image, blooddrop.gif, and aligning it to the left.
3. Begin the body section by adding the heading, Annual Blood Drive. Format the heading to use the Heading 1 style, be left-aligned, and use the font color red.
4. Add an unordered list with the three list items, as shown in Figure 3-56. Use a square bullet type for the bullet.
5. Add a Heading 2 style heading, About Donating, and type the paragraph of text shown in Figure 3-56.
6. Add a Heading 2 style heading, When, and the paragraph as shown in Figure 3-56.
7. Add a Heading 2 style heading, Contacts, and the paragraph as shown in Figure 3-56.
8. Create a target at the top of the page named, totop.
9. Create a To top link at the bottom of the page, as shown in Figure 3-56. Set the link to direct to the totop target at the top of the page.
10. Save the HTML file in the Project03\IntheLab folder using the file name, lab3-1solution.htm.
11. Print the lab3-1solution.htm file.
12. Enter the URL, `a:\Project03\IntheLab\lab3-1solution.htm`, to view the Web page in your browser.
13. Print the Web page.
14. Write your name on both printouts and hand them in to your instructor.

2 Creating a Web Page with Wrapped Text

Problem: You are the head of an after school volunteer program and decide to prepare a Web page announcement inviting people to join the group (Figure 3-57 on the next page). You decide to create a Web page with text wrapped around a left-aligned image to provide visual appeal.

(continued)

Creating a Web Page with Wrapped Text *(continued)*

FIGURE 3-57

Instructions: Start Notepad. Perform the following tasks using a computer:

1. Start a new HTML file with the title, Lab 3-2 [your name], in the main heading section.
2. Add a background image to the Web page using the greyback.jpg image.
3. Begin the body section by adding the Heading 1 style heading, AFTER SCHOOL PROGRAM, using a centered, italicized, blue font. Insert a break <br /> tag and add the heading, VOLUNTEERS NEEDED!, using the same formatting as the previous heading. (*Hint*: use the word blue for the color code.)
4. Add a size 10 horizontal rule below the heading.
5. Add the image, school.jpg, using attributes so it is left-aligned with horizontal space of 10, height of 226, and width of 324. Left-alignment will wrap text to the right of the image.
6. Add the paragraphs of information as shown in Figure 3-57.
7. Add an italicized e-mail sentence at the bottom of the paragraph and create the e-mail link as shown in Figure 3-57.

8. Save the HTML file in the Project03\IntheLab folder using the file name, lab3-2solution.htm.
9. Print the lab3-2solution.htm file.
10. Enter the URL, a:\Project03\IntheLab\lab3-2solution.htm, to view the Web page in your browser.
11. Print the Web page.
12. Write your name on the printouts and hand them in to your instructor.

3 Composing Two Linked Web Pages

Problem: Your English Composition instructor has asked each student in the class to create a two-page Web site to help other students in the class get to know them. She suggested using the basic template shown in Figures 3-58a and 3-58b on the next page as a starting point. The first Web page (Figure 3-58a) is a home page that includes basic personal information and a link to the second Web page. The second Web page (Figure 3-58b) includes a paragraph of text and a numbered list with links.

Instructions: Start Notepad. Perform the following steps using a computer:

1. Start a new HTML file with the title, Lab 3-3 [your name], in the main heading section.
2. In the first Web page, include a Heading style 1 heading, similar to the one shown in Figure 3-58a, and a short paragraph of text.
3. Create a text link to the second Web page, lab3-3favorites.htm.
4. Save the HTML file in the Project03\IntheLab folder using the file name, lab3-3solution.htm. Print the lab3-3solution.htm file.
5. Start a new HTML file with the title, Lab 3-3 Favorites [your name], in the main heading section.
6. In the second Web page, include a Heading style 1 heading, similar to the one shown in Figure 3-58b, a short paragraph of text, and two Heading style 2 headings. Create two ordered (numbered) lists with at least two items that serve as links to Web pages on another Web site.
7. Save the HTML file in the Project03\IntheLab folder using the file name, lab3-3favorites.htm. Print the lab3-3favorites.htm file.
8. Enter the URL, a:\Project03\IntheLab\lab3-3solution.htm, to view the Web page in your browser. Click the text link to the second Web page. Click the links in the lists to test them.
9. Print the Web pages.
10. Write your name on the printouts and hand them in to your instructor.

(continued)

Composing Two Linked Web Pages *(continued)*

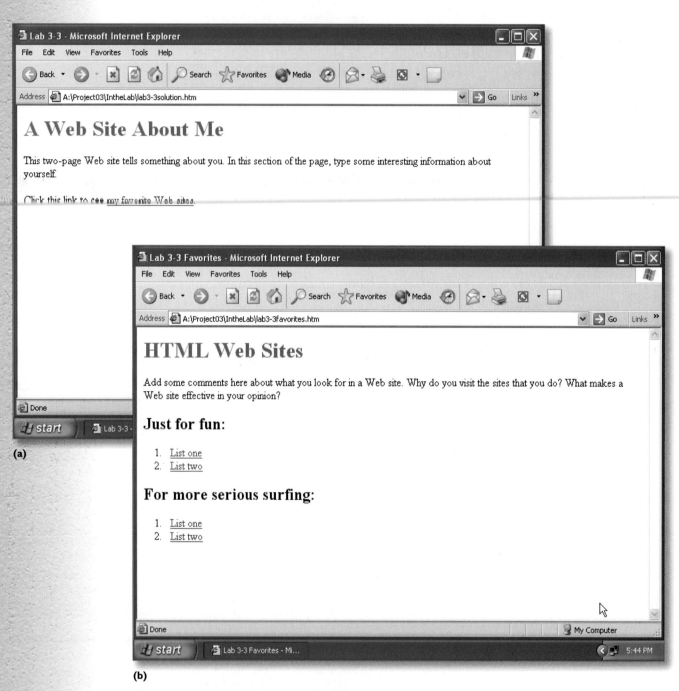

(a)

(b)

FIGURE 3-58

Cases and Places

The difficulty of these case studies varies:
■ are the least difficult and ■■ are the most difficult. The last exercise is a group exercise.

1 ■ Jared Smith is very impressed with the Plant World Web pages and now would like to add a Web page listing online gardening resources. Search the Web to find at least four Web sites that contain information about plants and gardening. Create a Web page that includes a Heading 1 style heading, a brief paragraph of descriptive text, and list links to those Web sites. Use the greyback.jpg background image in the new Web page, so all of the pages in the Web site look consistent. Modify the Plant World home page to include a link to the new Web page.

2 ■ Your manager at LightSpace Photography has asked you to update the home page to make it more visually appealing. As a first step, you plan to create a Web page with sample text formats, such as the ones shown in Figure 3-27 on page HTM 97, to share with your manager and get his input on which types of formatting he prefers. Create such a Web page and include text formatted as bold, italic, underlined, superscript, and subscript; use different colors and sizes for each type of text. Be sure to include one sample using the <bold> tag and one using the <strong> tag to see how they compare when displayed together.

3 ■■ To update the Plant World Web site further, you want to add image links so the plant images on the Desert Plants Web page also are links to Web pages in an external Web site. Search the Web for information specific to each of the four desert plants used in the project. Modify the Desert Plants Web page so each plant image is used as a link to a Web page in an external Web site. After adding the links, you decide the text paragraphs on the page are too close to the pictures. Modify the Desert Plants Web page to use the <img> tag attributes hspace and vspace to add space around each image.

4 ■■ The Marketing Director at Steel Solutions is unhappy the links on the company Web pages appear in blue when unvisited and purple when visited, because those are the logo colors of Steel Solutions' closest competitor. She has asked you to update the Web pages to use navy for unvisited links, olive for visited links, and red for active links. Create a Web page similar to Figure 3-4 on page HTM 73, with three text links to a Web page in an external Web site. Add the appropriate link attributes in the body tag to define the link colors as requested by the Marketing Director.

5 ■■ **Working Together** Your manager at Axcelent has asked your team to create a simple five-page prototype of the Web pages in the new Entertainment section for the online magazine, CityStuff. The home page should include headings and brief paragraphs of text for Arts, Music, Movies, and Dining. Within each paragraph of text is a link to one of the four detailed Web pages for each section (for example, the Arts link should connect to the Arts Web page). The home page also includes an e-mail link at the bottom of the page. Add a To top link that connects to a target at the top of the page. The four detailed Web pages should include links to external Web sites of interest and a link back to the home page. If possible, also find appropriate images to use as a background or in the Web page and set text to wrap around the images.

HTML

Creating Tables in a Web Site

CASE PERSPECTIVE

The city's newest video rental store, Bell Video, is having trouble attracting new customers. As advertising director for Bell Video, you are trying to think of new ways to promote three key differentiating features of Bell Video: excellent customer service, low rental prices, and a wide selection of videos. In researching the subject, you find many articles and case studies in which companies learned that having a solid Web site made it easier for customers to find them, provided a way to communicate the company's brand, and allowed the company to provide additional services. As you begin to understand the importance of the Web to businesses like your own, your recommendation is to create a Web site for Bell Video to help increase the store's exposure to current and new customers.

One of the services you want to provide on the Bell Video Web site is a way for customers to browse through the store's database of videos. In designing the various ways customers will be able to browse the database, you consider the questions that customers ask about videos when they visit the store. Sometimes, customers want to know about new releases. Other times, they do not know the name of the movie, but do know one or more actors in the movie. Finally, customers sometimes want to select a certain type of movie, such as comedy or action, rather than a specific movie. Given that, you design three Web pages to allow customers to browse by new releases, by actor, or by type. You decide to develop the necessary Web pages with this information to show at the next staff meeting, so you can gather feedback from the team.

As you read through this project, you will learn how to plan, design, and code a table to create a user-friendly Web site. You also will learn to format tables and to combine table features to make the pages more readable. In addition, you will learn to create a menu bar with text links.

HTML

Creating Tables in a Web Site

Objectives

You will have mastered the material in this project when you can:

- Define table elements
- Describe the steps used to plan, design, and code a table
- Create a borderless table to organize images
- Create a vertical menu bar with text links
- Create a borderless table to organize text
- Create a horizontal menu bar with text links
- Create a table with borders
- Change the horizontal alignment of text
- Add background color to rows and cells
- Alter the spacing between and within cells using the cellspacing and cellpadding attributes
- Insert a caption below a table
- Use the rowspan and colspan attributes

Introduction

In the first three projects, you learned the fundamentals of Web page development, as well as how to create an HTML file and use paragraphs and lists of text items to present information on a Web page. This project adds to your HTML knowledge by teaching you how to present information on a Web page using tables with rows and columns. In this project, you will learn about the elements used in a table and how to plan, design, and code a table. You also will learn how to create tables to organize text and images and to use a table column to create a menu bar with text links. The project also discusses how to enhance tables by using a variety of attributes and formats, such as borders, colors, spacing, and blank cells, and by adding a caption to the table.

Project Four — Bell Video

When a Web page is developed, tables often are used to organize and position text and images to help make the Web pages look more organized and professional. Project 4 illustrates how to create two pages for the Bell Video Web site, including a home page and the New Releases Web page, and how to edit two existing pages, including the Actor and Type Web pages.

As shown in Figure 4-1a, the Bell Video home page includes a borderless table to position two images at the top of the page, as well as a second borderless table that organizes text and a vertical menu bar of text links that link to the other three Web pages.

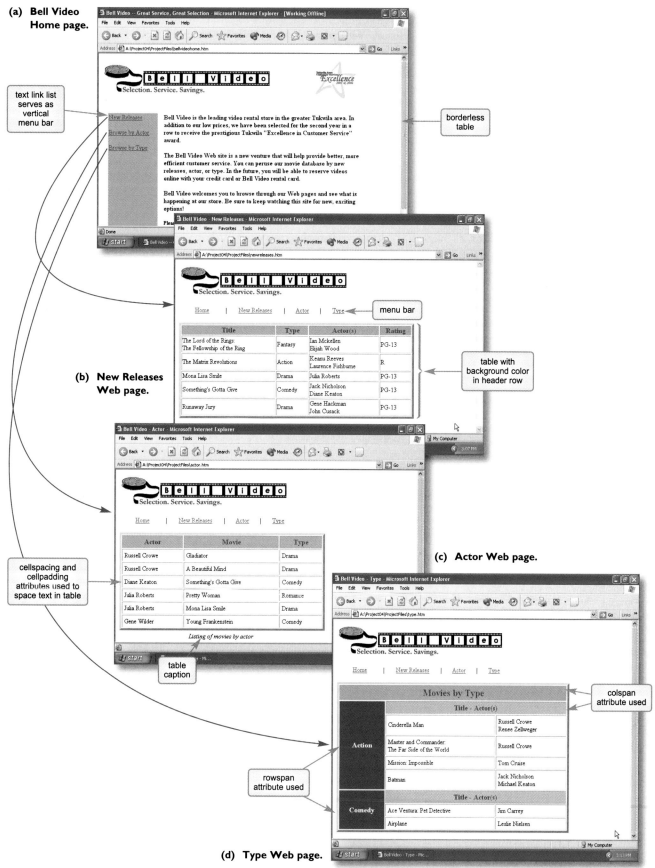

(a) Bell Video Home page.

text link list serves as vertical menu bar

borderless table

(b) New Releases Web page.

menu bar

table with background color in header row

(c) Actor Web page.

cellspacing and cellpadding attributes used to space text in table

table caption

colspan attribute used

rowspan attribute used

(d) Type Web page.

FIGURE 4-1

The New Releases, Actor, and Type Web pages all include two borderless tables: one to position the logo image and the other to create a horizontal menu bar of text links. The New Releases Web page (Figure 4-1b on the previous page) also includes a table with a background color to highlight the table headings. The basic HTML for the Actor and Type Web pages is included on the HTML Data Disk. The Actor Web page (Figure 4-1c) is edited to use cellspacing and cellpadding attributes and a caption to give the table a different appearance. The Type Web page (Figure 4-1d) is edited to use the colspan and rowspan attributes to create headings that span several columns and rows. As shown in Figure 4-1, all three of these Web pages use vertical alignment and color in specific cells to enhance the appearance of the table.

Creating Web Pages with Tables

Tables allow you to organize information on a Web page using HTML tags. Tables are useful when you want to arrange text and images into rows and columns in order to make the information straightforward and clear to the Web page visitor. You can use tables to create Web pages with two newspaper-type columns of text or structured lists of information. Tables can be complex, using the rowspan and colspan attributes to span rows and columns, background colors in cells, and borders to provide formatting (Figure 4-2a). Tables also can be simple, with a basic grid format and no color (Figure 4-2b). The purpose of the table helps to define what formatting is appropriate.

(a) Complex table.

(b) Simple table.

FIGURE 4-2

Project 3 discussed wrapping text around an image. Tables also can be used to position text and images, such as the one shown in Figure 4-3, which uses a border-less table to position text to the left of the map images. An advantage to using a table to position text and images, instead of just wrapping the text around the image, is that you have more control over the placement of the text and image.

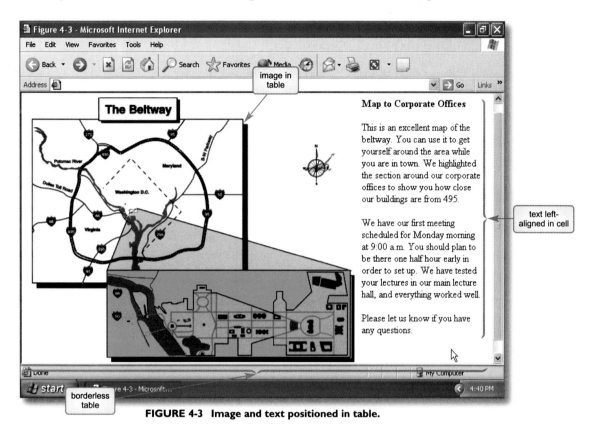

FIGURE 4-3 Image and text positioned in table.

Tables also can be used to create a border or frame around an image, as shown in Figure 4-4. The Web page shown in Figure 4-4 shows an image inserted into a table with one row and one cell. The border is set to a pixel width of 15 to create the appearance of a frame. Using a table to create a frame is a simple technique that gives an image a polished look and highlights the image.

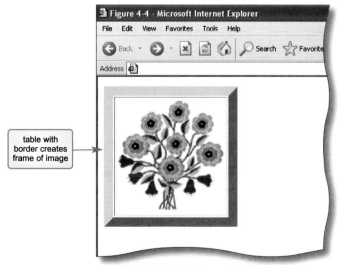

FIGURE 4-4 Table used as image frame.

Table Elements

Tables consist of rows, columns, and cells, much like spreadsheets. A **row** is a horizontal line of information. A **column** is a vertical line of information. A **cell** is the intersection of a row and a column. Figure 4-5 shows examples of these three elements. In Figure 4-5a, the fifth row in the table has a yellow background. In Figure 4-5b, the fourth column has a red background. In Figure 4-5c, the cell at the intersection of column 2 and row 2 has a lime green background.

As shown in Figure 4-5c, a cell can be one of two types: a heading cell or a data cell. A **heading cell** displays text as bold and center-aligned. A **data cell** displays normal text that is left-aligned.

Understanding the row, column, and cell elements is important, as you create a table using HTML. Attributes are set are relative to these table elements. For example, you can set attributes for an entire row of information, for a single cell, or for one or more cells within a row.

(a) Table with row background color.

(c) Table with cell background color.

(b) Table with column background color.

FIGURE 4-5

Table Borders, Headers, Captions, and Rules

Tables also include features such as table borders, table headers, table captions, and rules (Figure 4-6). A **table border** is the line that encloses the perimeter of the table. A **table header** is the same as a heading cell — that is, it is any cell with bold text that indicates the purpose of the row or column. A **table caption** is descriptive text located above or below the table that further describes the purpose of the table.

Tables can use each of these features or a combination of them. The purpose for the table dictates which of these features are used. For example, the table shown in Figure 4-6 lists columns of numbers. A header row is used to identify the meaning of the numbers in each column, and headings that span columns and rows are used to provide additional information. Finally, the table caption explains that each number is based on thousands (that is, the 10 listed in the table represents 10,000).

FIGURE 4-6 Table headers, border, and caption.

Another useful attribute of a table is the rules attribute. The **rules attribute** allows a Web developer to select which internal borders to show in a table. The rules attribute supports several values to provide different formatting options. For example, using the attribute and value rules="none" creates a table with no internal rules. Using the attribute and value rules="cols" creates a table with vertical rules between each column in the table (Figure 4-7a), while rules="rows" creates a table with horizontal rules between each row in the table (Figure 4-7b). Appendix A provides additional information on values supported by the rules attribute.

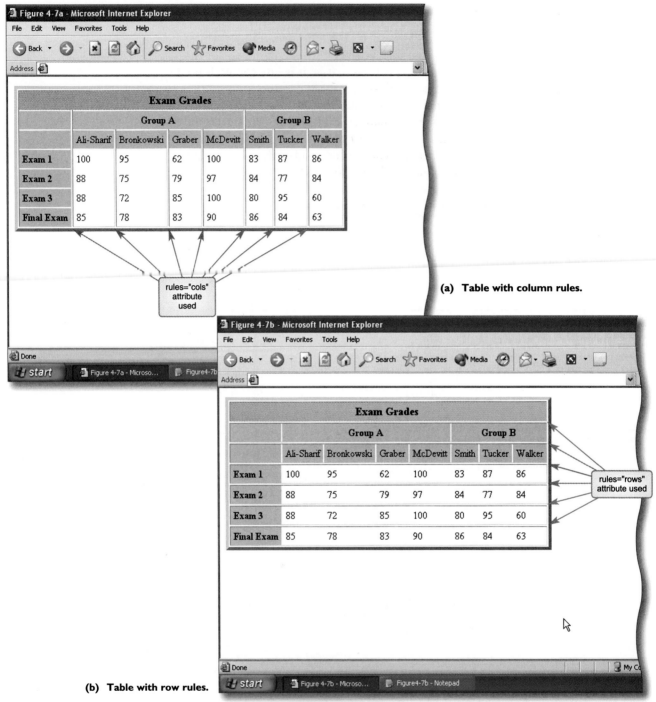

(a) Table with column rules.

(b) Table with row rules.

FIGURE 4-7

Planning, Designing, and Coding a Table

Creating tables for a Web page is a three-step process: (1) determining if a table is needed; (2) planning the table; and (3) coding the table. Each of these steps is discussed in detail in the following sections.

Determining if a Table Is Needed

First, you must determine whether or not a table is necessary. Not all Web pages require the use of tables. A general rule of thumb is that a table should be used when it will help organize information or Web page elements in such a way that it is easier for the Web page visitor to read. Tables generally are useful in a Web page if the Web page needs to display a structured, organized list of information or includes text and images that must be positioned in a very specific manner. Figure 4-8 shows an example of information displayed as text in both a table and a bulleted list. To present this information, a table might be the better choice. The bulleted list might give the Web page an acceptable look, but the table more clearly explains the topic.

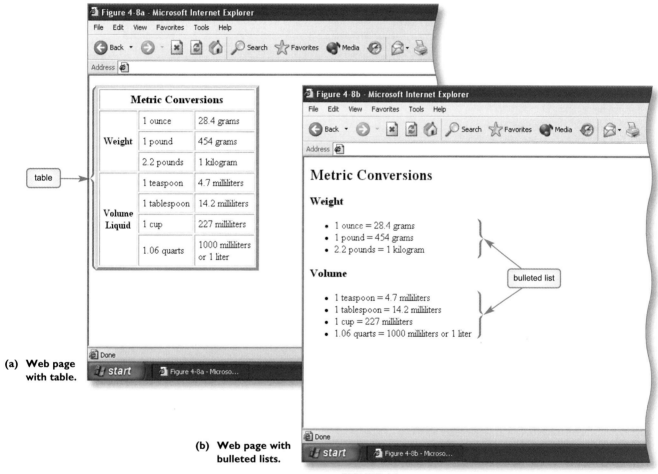

(a) Web page with table.

(b) Web page with bulleted lists.

FIGURE 4-8

Planning the Table

In order to create effective tables, you must begin by planning how the information will display in the table and create a good design. Before writing any HTML code, sketch the table out on paper. After the table is sketched on paper, it is easier to see how many rows and columns to create, if the table will include headings, and if any of the headings span rows or columns. Conceptualizing the table on paper first saves time trying to determine which HTML table tags to use to create the table.

For example, to create a simple table that lists the times run by various cross-country team members, you might sketch the table shown in Figure 4-9a on the next page. If runners participate in two different race lengths, such as 5K and 10K, that information can be included in a table designed as shown in Figure 4-9b. If the table needs to include different race dates for each race length, that information can be included in a table such as the one shown in Figure 4-9c. Finally, to make the table easier for the Web page visitor to understand, the table should include headings that span rows and columns and a caption, as shown in Figure 4-10. Design issues such as these should be considered while planning the table, before any HTML code is entered.

NAME1	NAME2	NAME3	NAME4
TIME	TIME	TIME	TIME

(a) Simple Table

5K		10K	
NAME1	NAME2	NAME3	NAME4
TIME	TIME	TIME	TIME

(b) Column Spanning Added

	5K		10K	
	NAME1	NAME2	NAME3	NAME4
MAY 5	TIME	TIME	TIME	TIME
MAY 12	TIME	TIME	TIME	TIME
MAY 19	TIME	TIME	TIME	TIME
MAY 26	TIME	TIME	TIME	TIME

(c) Row Spanning Added

FIGURE 4-9

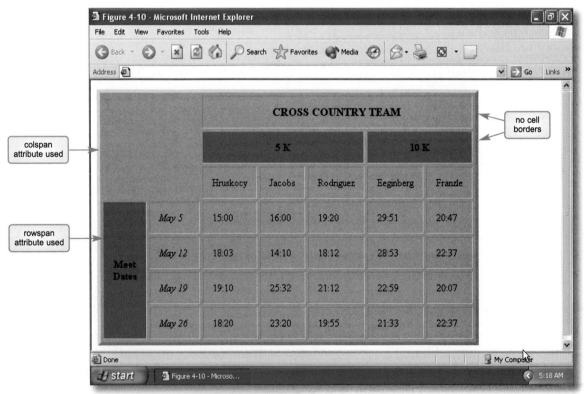

FIGURE 4-10 Table with row and column spanning.

Coding the Table

After the table design is complete, the table can be coded using HTML tags. Table 4-1 shows the four main HTML tags used to create a table. Each of these tags has a number of attributes, which are discussed later in this project.

Table 4-1 HTML Table Tags	
TAG	FUNCTION
<table> </table>	• Indicates the start and end of a table • All other table tags are inserted within these tags
<tr> </tr>	• Indicates the start and end of a table row • Rows consist of heading or data cells
<th> </th>	• Indicates the start and end of a table heading (also called a heading cell) • Table headings default to bold text and center-alignment
<td> </td>	• Indicates the start and end of a data cell in a table • Data cells default to normal text and left-alignment

Figure 4-11a on the next page shows an example of these tags used in an HTML file and Figure 4-11b shows the resulting Web page. As shown in Figure 4-11b, the table has four rows (a table header and three rows of data cells) and two columns. The rows are indicated in the HTML file in Figure 4-11a by the start **<tr>** tags and the end **</tr>** tags. For this simple table, the number of columns in the table is determined based on the number of cells within each row. As shown in Figure 4-11b, each row has two cells, which results in a table with two columns. (Later in the project, you will learn how to indicate the number of columns within the <table> tag.)

As shown in the HTML in Figure 4-11a, the first row includes table heading cells, as indicated by the start **<th>** tag and end **</th>** tag. In the second, third, and fourth rows, the cells contain data, indicated by the start **<td>** tag and end **</td>** tag. In the resulting table, as shown in Figure 4-11b, the table header in row 1 displays bold and centered text. The text in the data cells in rows 2 through 4 is left-aligned and normal. The table in Figure 4-11b is borderless, because no border attribute was specified in the <table> tag. Cellspacing of 15 pixels was added to further highlight the differences between the cells.

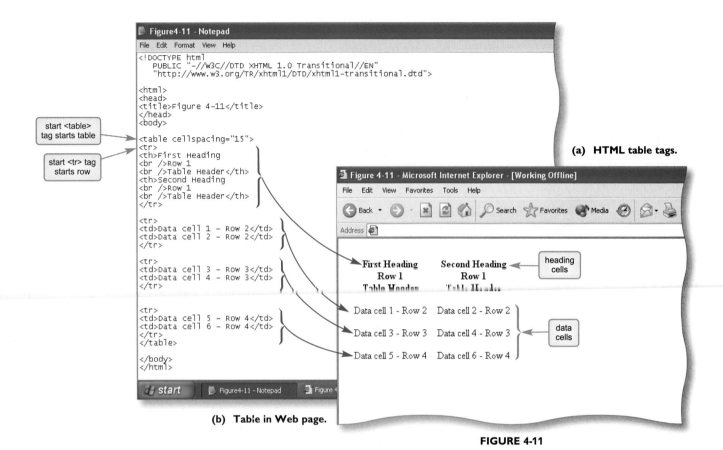

FIGURE 4-11

Table Tag Attributes

Each of the four main table tags listed in Table 4-1 has different attributes. Table 4-2 lists these tags and the main attributes associated with each tag. The <th> and <td> tags, which both are used to specify the contents of a cell, have the same attributes. Many of the table tags and attributes listed below are used in this project to create the Bell Video Web site.

Table 4-2 Table Tag Attributes and Functions

TAG	ATTRIBUTE	FUNCTION
<table> </table>	align	• Controls table alignment (left, center, right)
	bgcolor	• Sets background color for table
	border	• Defines width of table border in pixels
	cellspacing	• Defines space between cells in pixels
	cellpadding	• Defines space within cells in pixels
	cols	• Defines number of columns
	width	• Sets table width relative to window width
<tr> </tr>	align	• Horizontally aligns row (left, center, right, justify)
	bgcolor	• Sets background color for row
	valign	• Vertically aligns row (top, middle, bottom)
<th> </th> and <td> </td>	align	• Horizontally aligns cell (left, center, right, justify)
	bgcolor	• Sets background color for cell
	colspan	• Sets number of columns spanned by a cell
	rowspan	• Sets number of rows spanned by a cell
	valign	• Vertically aligns cell (top, middle, bottom)

Creating a Home Page

The first Web page developed in this project is the home page of the Bell Video Web site. As you have learned, the home page is the main page of a Web site, which Web site visitors generally view first. Visitors then click links to move from the home page to the other Web pages in the site. The Bell Video home page includes three links to other pages: the New Releases Web page, the Actor Web page, and the Type Web page. The home page also provides an e-mail link, so visitors easily can find contact information for Bell Video.

Starting Notepad

The first step in creating the Bell Video Web site is to start Notepad. The following steps show how to start Notepad and maximize the window.

To Start Notepad

1 Click the Start button on the taskbar.

2 Point to All Programs on the Start menu, point to Accessories on the All Programs submenu, and then click Notepad on the Accessories submenu.

3 If the Notepad window is not maximized, click the Maximize button on the Notepad title bar to maximize it.

4 Click Format on the menu bar and, if necessary, click Word Wrap to turn Word Wrap on.

The Notepad window is displayed and Word Wrap is enabled.

Entering HTML Tags to Define the Web Page Structure

As you have learned, every HTML file includes HTML tags that define the overall structure of a standard Web page and divide the HTML file into its basic sections. Table 4-3 shows the HTML tags entered to define the structure of the Bell Video home page. The following steps show how to enter the HTML tags that define the structure of the Bell Video home page.

LINE	HTML TAG AND TEXT
Table 4-3	HTML Code to Define Web Page Structure
1	`<!DOCTYPE html`
2	`    PUBLIC "-//W3C//DTD XHTML 1.0 Transitional//EN"`
3	`    "http://www.w4.org/TR/xhtml1/DTD/xhtml1-transitional.dtd">`
4	
5	`<html>`
6	`<head>`
7	`<title>Bell Video -- Great Service, Great Selection</title>`
8	`</head>`
9	`<body>`
10	
11	`</body>`
12	`</html>`

To Enter HTML Tags to Define the Web Page Structure

1 **Enter the HTML code as shown in Table 4-3.**

Notepad displays the HTML code (Figure 4-12).

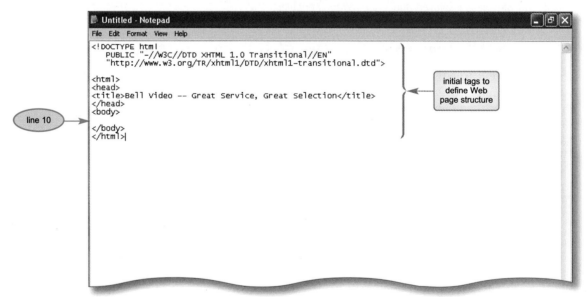

FIGURE 4-12

Using Borderless Tables to Position Images

Next, a borderless table is added to the Bell Video home page, in order to position the Bell Video logo image and the customer service excellence image at the top of the Web page (Figure 4-13).

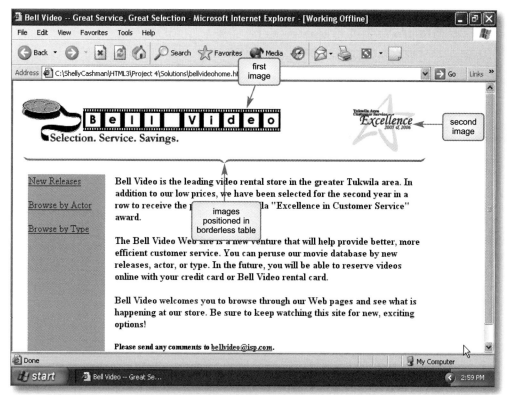

FIGURE 4-13 Bell Video Home page.

The HTML code to create a borderless table as shown in Figure 4-13 is as follows:

```
<table border="0" cols="2" width="90%">
```

where the border="0" attribute creates a borderless table, the cols="2" attribute indicates two columns are in the table, and the width="90%" indicates that the table should utilize 90% of the window's width. A benefit of using a percentage to set the table width is that it automatically changes the width of the table if the window is resized in the browser.

Figure 4-14a on the next page shows a sample of a table with the attributes border="2" and width="80%". The bordered table appears center-aligned on the Web page and utilizes 80% of the window's width. Figure 4-14b shows the same table with align="left", border="2", and width="100%" attributes. The bordered table appears left-aligned on the Web page and utilizes 100% of the window's width. Figure 4-14c shows the same table, with no attributes specified. The table uses the default left-alignment and appears with no borders. Because no width is specified, the table utilizes 100% of the window's width.

FIGURE 4-14

Creating a Borderless Table to Position Images

Using these attributes, perform the steps on the next page to insert the heading table.

To Create a Borderless Table to Position Images

1

• If necessary, click line 10.

2

• **Type** <table border="0" cols="2" width="90%"> and then press the ENTER key.

The <table> tag is displayed (Figure 4-15).

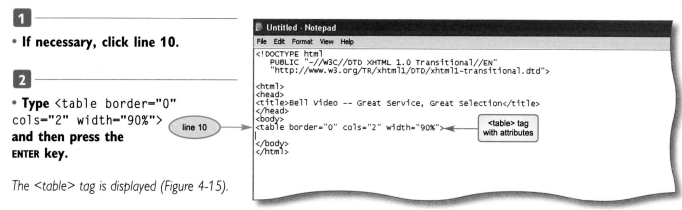

FIGURE 4-15

Inserting Images in a Table

The table shown in Figure 4-13 on page HTM 145 contains one row with two data cells in the row. The first data cell contains the image, bellvideologo.gif, and the second data cell contains the image, csexcellence.gif. To create data cells in a row, the HTML tags must include one or more sets of <td> </td> tags between the <tr> </tr> tags. Recall that the <tr> tag means table row, and the <td> tag means table data cell. Adding two sets of <td> </td> tags creates two data cells, one for each image. Data cell (<td> </td>) tags are used, rather than header cell (<th> </th>) tags, so that the image files can be left-aligned in the cell, instead of using the default center-alignment for heading cells. The following steps illustrate how to insert images in a table.

To Insert Images in a Table

1

• If necessary, click line 11, type <tr> as the tag, and then press the ENTER key.

• **Type** <td><img src="bellvideologo.gif" width="430" height="74" alt="Bell Video Logo" /> </td> **and then press the ENTER key.**

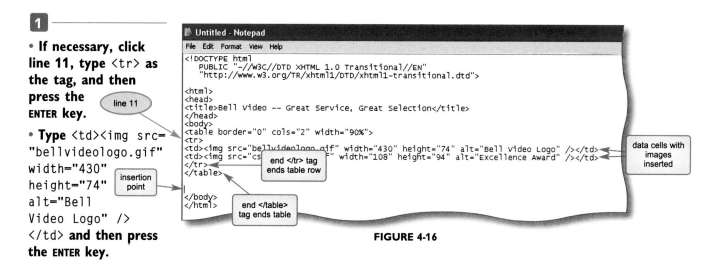

FIGURE 4-16

2

• **Type** <td><img src="csexcellence.gif" width="108" height="94" alt="Excellence Award" /></td> **and then press the ENTER key.**

3

• **Type** `</tr>` **and then press the ENTER key.**

4

• **Type** `</table>` **and then press the ENTER key twice.**

The HTML code is displayed (Figure 4-16).

The first table on the Bell Video home page is complete. The HTML code entered creates a borderless table that includes two images, bellvideologo.gif and csexcellence.gif, which are included on the HTML Data Disk. The attributes specified for the images indicate alt text and the height and width of these images in pixels. As you have learned, indicating the width and height of an image takes the burden off of the browser in calculating those dimensions and thus helps Web pages load faster. Later in the project, this HTML code is copied for use on the other three Web pages.

FIGURE 4-17

Creating a Vertical Menu Bar with Text Links

The Web site created in this project consists of four Web pages. Visitors should be able to move easily from one Web page to any of the other three Web pages. Providing a menu bar, either on the left side or top of the Web page, prevents the visitor from having to search the page for navigation links.

The following section shows how to create a one-row, two-column, borderless table, as shown in Figure 4-17a. The left column of the table is used to create a vertical menu bar of text links to the other three Web pages. The right column of the table is used to display text describing Bell Video.

To format the table as shown in Figure 4-17a, the cellspacing attribute in the <table> tag is used to insert some space between the left and right columns in the table. The **cellspacing** attribute sets the amount of space between cells. Figure 4-17a shows the home page with cellspacing used; Figure 4-17b shows the same page without cellspacing. As shown in these figures, the two columns are too close together when cellspacing is not used. Using cellspacing adds space between cells (or columns), which gives the table additional white space and creates a more polished look.

To create the table shown in Figure 4-17a, the <table> tag is used, along with four table attributes, as shown in Table 4-4.

Table 4-4 HTML Code to Create a Vertical Menu Bar of Text Links	
LINE	**HTML TAG AND TEXT**
17	` <table border="0" cellspacing="15" cols="2" width="90%">`
18	`<tr>`
19	`<td valign="top" width="20%" bgcolor="lightsteelblue">`
20	`<a href="newreleases.htm">New Releases</a>`
21	
22	`<p><a href="actor.htm">Browse by Actor</a></p>`
23	
24	`<p><a href="type.htm">Browse by Type</a></p>`
25	`</td>`

Line 17 creates a table, where the border="0" attribute creates a borderless table, the cols="2" attribute indicates two columns are in the table, cellspacing="15" adds 15 pixels of space between table cells, width="90%" indicates that the table should display in 90% of the window's width, and align="center" centers the table on the Web page. The break tag <br /> at the beginning of the second table provides space between the two borderless tables. As in the first table, the width attribute sets the width of the entire table to a percentage of the window's width. This table also is set at 90%.

The columns of cells in the table are data cells, used to organize text and text links. The default vertical alignment for data cells is centered. As shown in Figure 4-17a, in this table, the text in the data cells should be aligned with the top of the cell. To change the alignment, the **valign="top"** attribute is used in the <tr> tag for the row (line 19). Using the valign="top" attribute aligns the information at the top of the cell. Vertical alignment also can be set in each individual cell of a row by using the **valign** attribute in the <td> tags in the row. If you want to set the vertical alignment for the entire row, using the valign attribute of the <tr> tag is more efficient.

Line 19 also shows the **bgcolor** attribute within the <td> tag of the first cell, which sets the background color for the first cell to light steel blue and provides a background for the menu bar. As with the valign attribute, the bgcolor attribute also can be used in the <tr> tag to set the background color for the entire row, instead of a specific cell.

Finally, the table in Figure 4-17a uses the **width** attribute within the <td> tag of each cell, to indicate the width of each column relative to the entire table. Columns of information in a table do not have to be equal widths, which allows the table to be formatted to organize text and images of different lengths and sizes. For example, in this table, the left column is set to 20% of the table width to contain short lines of text used as text links in a menu bar (lines 20 through 24). The right column will be set to 80% of the table width to contain paragraphs of text. The width attribute provides the flexibility to vary column widths in cases such as this. The width attribute of the <td> tag can be used to set the width to a specific number of pixels or as a percentage of the width of the table. Setting the width as a percentage is recommended, so that column widths are changed if the window is resized in the browser.

The following steps show how to create a borderless table and a vertical menu bar with text links.

To Create a Vertical Menu Bar with Text Links

1 If necessary, click line 17 (Figure 4-18).

2 Enter the HTML code as shown in Table 4-4 on the previous page.

3 Press the ENTER key twice.

The HTML code to create a borderless table with three text links is displayed (Figure 4-18).

FIGURE 4-18

The previous steps created a two-column, borderless table that is center-aligned and has cellspacing of 15 pixels between columns. The table was set to fill 90% of the window's width. The HTML code shown in Figure 4-18 also formatted the first data cell to be 20% of the table's width and use a light steel blue background color. Three links then were included in that data cell, to provide a vertical menu bar of links to the other three Web pages in the Web site. The vertical menu bar in the left column of this table allows the visitor to move from the home page to any other page quickly. Figure 4-19 shows the results of your work so far.

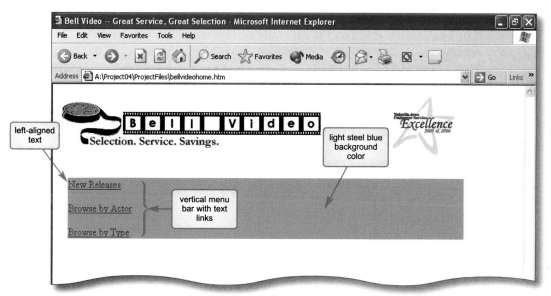

FIGURE 4-19 Web page with one-column table.

Adding Text to a Table Cell

Next, the paragraph of text must be added in the right column of the table, as shown in Figure 4-17a on page HTM 148. Table 4-5 shows the HTML code used to create a second column in the table, add text including an e-mail link, and then end the table.

LINE	HTML TAG AND TEXT
	Table 4-5 HTML Code to Add Text to a Table Cell
27	`<td valign=top width="80%"><b>Bell Video is the leading video rental store`
28	`in the greater Tukwila area. In addition to our low prices, we have been`
29	`selected for the second year in a row to receive the prestigious Tukwila`
30	`"Excellence in Customer Service" award.`
31	
32	`<p>The Bell Video Web site is a new venture that will help provide better,`
33	`more efficient customer service. You can peruse our movie database by new`
34	`releases, actor, or type. In the future, you will be able to reserve videos online`
35	`with your credit card or Bell Video rental card.</p>`
36	
37	`<p>Bell Video welcomes you to browse through our Web pages and see what is`
38	`happening at our store. Be sure to keep watching this site for new, exciting`
39	`options!</p>`
40	
41	`<p><font size="-1">Please send any comments to <a`
42	`href="mailto:bellvideo@isp.com">bellvideo@isp.com</a>.</font></p></b>`
43	`</td>`
44	`</tr>`
45	`</table>`

As shown in Table 4-5 on the previous page, the second column is created using the set of <td> </td> tags. The HTML code of the paragraph text and e-mail link then are inserted within the <td> </td> tags. To create blank lines, as shown in lines 31, 36, and 40, press the ENTER key twice after typing lines 30, 35, and 39.

The following steps illustrate how to add text to a table cell.

To Add Text to a Table Cell

1 If necessary, click line 27.

2 Enter the HTML code as shown in Table 4-5 and then press the ENTER key.

The HTML code is displayed (Figure 4-20).

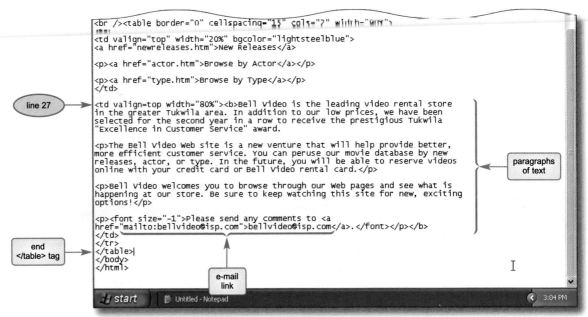

FIGURE 4-20

As shown in Figure 4-20, the <td> </td> tags create a new data cell set to 80% of the table's width. The <td> </td> tags enclose four paragraphs of text, including an e-mail link to bellvideo@isp.com. Finally, lines 43 through 45 end the current cell, the current row, and the table. The next step is to save and print the HTML file.

The HTML code for the Bell Video home page is complete. The Web page includes two tables used to organize images and text. The first table is a borderless, one-row, two-column table containing two images. The second is a borderless, one-row, two-column table containing text. The left column uses a background color to highlight a vertical menu bar of text links to the other Web pages in the Web site. The right column contains text describing Bell Video.

Two tables were used in the Bell Video home page, so that each table could be set to a different width. In the first table, the total width of the table is 80%. In the second table, the total width is 90%. The widths of the two columns in the second table are 20% of the table width and 70% of the table width, respectively.

With the HTML code for the Bell Video home page complete, the file should be saved and a copy should be printed as a reference.

To Save and Print the HTML File

1 With a floppy disk in drive A, click File on the menu bar and then click Save As. Type `bellvideohome.htm` in the File name text box.

2 If necessary, click 3½ Floppy (A:) in the Save in list. Click the Project04 folder and then click the ProjectFiles folder in the list of available folders. Click the Save button in the Save As dialog box.

3 Click File on the menu bar and then click Print on the File menu.

Notepad saves the HTML file in the Project04\ProjectFiles folder on the floppy disk in drive A using the file name, bellvideohome.htm. Notepad prints the HTML file (Figure 4-21).

```
<!DOCTYPE html
    PUBLIC "-//W3C//DTD XHTML 1.0 Transitional//EN"
    "http://www.w3.org/TR/xhtml1/DTD/xhtml1-transitional.dtd">

<html>
<head>
<title>Bell Video -- Great Service, Great Selection</title>
</head>
<body>
<table border="0" cols="2" width="90%">
<tr>
<td><img src="bellvideologo.gif" width="430" height="74" alt="Bell Video Logo" /></td>
<td><img src="csexcellence.gif" width="108" height="94" alt="Excellence Award" /></td>
</tr>
</table>

<br /><table border="0" cellspacing="15" cols="2" width="90%">
<tr>
<td valign="top" width="20%" bgcolor="lightsteelblue">
<a href="newreleases.htm">New Releases</a>

<p><a href="actor.htm">Browse by Actor</a></p>

<p><a href="type.htm">Browse by Type</a></p>
</td>

<td valign=top width="80%"><b>Bell Video is the leading video rental store
in the greater Tukwila area. In addition to our low prices, we have been
selected for the second year in a row to receive the prestigious Tukwila
"Excellence in Customer Service" award.

<p>The Bell Video Web site is a new venture that will help provide better,
more efficient customer service. You can peruse our movie database by new
releases, actor, or type. In the future, you will be able to reserve videos
online with your credit card or Bell Video rental card.</p>

<p>Bell Video welcomes you to browse through our Web pages and see what is
happening at our store. Be sure to keep watching this site for new, exciting
options!</p>

<p><font size="-1">Please send any comments to <a
href="mailto:bellvideo@isp.com">bellvideo@isp.com</a>.</font></p></b>
</td>
</tr>
</table>

</body>
</html>
```

FIGURE 4-21

Viewing and Printing the Web Page Using the Browser

After the HTML file for the Bell Video home page is saved, it should be viewed in a browser to confirm that the Web page appears as desired and that the links function as expected. To test the Bell Video home page, click the e-mail link to verify that it works correctly. Next, click each of the three vertical menu bar links. Clicking the New Releases link will display a blank page, as that Web page is developed later in the project. Clicking the Actor and Type links will display the Actor and Type Web pages, which are stored on the HTML Data Disk as they are developed thus far. Later in the project, edits will be made to both the Actor and Type Web pages.

The following steps show how to view and print the Web page.

To View and Print a Web Page

1

• **Click the Start button on the Windows taskbar and then point to All Programs on the Start menu.**

• **Click Internet Explorer (or another browser command) on the All Programs submenu.**

• **If necessary, click the Maximize button to maximize the browser window.**

2

• **Type** a:\Project04\ ProjectFiles\ bellvideohome.htm **in the Address text box and then press the ENTER key.**

FIGURE 4-22

The Bell Video home page is displayed (Figure 4-22).

3

• **Click the Print button on the Standard Buttons toolbar.**

The home page prints (Figure 4-23).

Selection. Service. Savings.

New Releases

Browse by Actor

Browse by Type

Bell Video is the leading video rental store in the greater Tukwila area. In addition to our low prices, we have been selected for the second year in a row to receive the prestigious Tukwila "Excellence in Customer Service" award.

The Bell Video Web site is a new venture that will help provide better, more efficient customer service. You can peruse our movie database by new releases, actor, or type. In the future, you will be able to reserve videos online with your credit card or Bell Video rental card.

Bell Video welcomes you to browse through our Web pages and see what is happening at our store. Be sure to keep watching this site for new, exciting options!

Please send any comments to bellvideo@isp.com.

FIGURE 4-23

The home page is complete. The next step is to create the New Releases Web page with two tables: one to create a horizontal menu bar and another to organize a list of text.

Creating a Secondary Web Page

As previously discussed, it is important to give Web site visitors the option to move easily from one Web page to another without having to search for links. The Bell Video home page includes a vertical menu bar of text links to meet this need. The three remaining Web pages in the Bell Video Web site include a horizontal menu bar of text links, positioned toward the top of the Web page, just after the header table.

Figure 4-24 shows the New Releases Web page with a horizontal menu bar of text links. The menu bar lists the four Web pages — Home, New Releases, Actor, and Type — with a | (pipe) symbol between the four links.

FIGURE 4-24 New Releases Web page.

To provide consistency throughout the Web site, as shown in Figure 4-1 on page HTM 133, the Bell Video logo should appear at the top of each Web page. The first steps in creating the New Releases Web page, as shown in Figure 4-24, thus is to add the HTML tags to define the Web page structure and create a borderless table with a Bell Video logo image. Recall that the Bell Video home page uses a borderless table with the Bell Video logo image and the customer service excellence image. Rather than entering this code again, the code from the Bell Video home page can be copied and pasted into the HTML file for the New Releases Web page and then edited to delete the image, csexcellence.gif. The following steps show how to copy the header table from the HTML file, bellvideohome.htm, to a new HTML file.

To Copy and Paste HTML Code to a New File

1 Click the Notepad button on the taskbar.

2 Click immediately to the left of the < in the <!DOCTYPE html tag on line 1. Drag through the first </table> tag on line 15 to highlight lines 1 through 15.

3 Press CTRL+C to copy the selected lines to the Clipboard.

4 Click File on the menu bar and then click New.

5 Press CTRL+V to paste the contents from the Clipboard into a new file.

The HTML code for the new file is displayed (Figure 4-25).

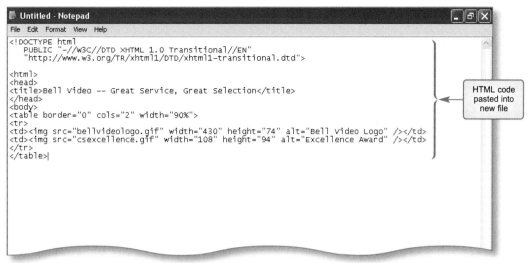

FIGURE 4-25

Changing the Title

The next step is to edit the pasted code to change the title of the Web page and delete the image, csexcellence.gif. The title of the Web page should be changed to Bell Video - New Releases, so that the title of the current Web page is displayed on the title bar of the Web browser.

The following steps show how to change the title of the Web page.

To Change the Title

1 Highlight the words, -- Great Service, Great Selection, between the <title> and </title> tags on line 7. Type - New Releases as the text.

2 Click immediately to the right of the </table> tag on line 15. Press the ENTER key three times.

3 Type </body> and then press the ENTER key.

4 Type </html> as the end tag.

The HTML code is displayed (Figure 4-26).

FIGURE 4-26

Deleting an Image

The customer service award image also should be deleted from the New Releases Web page, so that the Web page appears as shown in Figure 4-24 on page HTM 156. Because the New Releases Web page has a horizontal menu bar, including the customer service award image makes the Web page look very cluttered. Removing the customer service award image by deleting line 13 of the HTML code results in a more polished Web page.

The following steps show to delete the line of HTML code that inserts the customer service award image.

To Delete an Image

1. **Highlight line 13, which contains the code to insert the image, csexcellence.gif.**

2. **Press the DELETE key twice.**

The Web page with the completed changes is displayed (Figure 4-27).

```
Untitled - Notepad
File   Edit   Format   View   Help
<!DOCTYPE html
    PUBLIC "-//W3C//DTD XHTML 1.0 Transitional//EN"
    "http://www.w3.org/TR/xhtml1/DTD/xhtml1-transitional.dtd">

<html>
<head>
<title>Bell Video - New Releases</title>
</head>
<body>
<table border="0" cols="1" width="10%">
<tr>
<td><img src="bellvideologo.gif" width="430" height="74" alt="Bell Video Logo" /></td>
</tr>
</table>


</body>
</html>
```

start   Untitled - Notepad   Bell Video -- Great Se...

FIGURE 4-27

Creating a Horizontal Menu Bar with Text Links

The next step in creating the New Releases Web page is to create a second borderless table that can be used as a horizontal menu bar, as shown in Figure 4-28 on page HTM 160. Table 4-6 lists the HTML tags and text are used to create the horizontal menu bar.

Table 4-6 HTML Code to Insert a Menu Bar

LINE	HTML TAG AND TEXT
16	` <table border="0" cols="7" width="60%">`
17	`<tr align="center">`
18	`<td width="20%"><a href="bellvideohome.htm">Home</a></td>`
19	`<td width="1%">|</td>`
20	`<td width="25%"><a href="newreleases.htm">New Releases</a></td>`
21	`<td width="1%">|</td>`
22	`<td width="15%"><a href="actor.htm">Actor</a></td>`
23	`<td width="1%">|</td>`
24	`<td width="15%"><a href="type.htm">Type</a></td>`
25	`</tr>`
26	`</table>`

The table created by the HTML code in Table 4-6 is a borderless, one-row, seven-column table. To improve the appearance of the Web page, the table is set to 60% of the window's width, so that it is not as wide as the first table. The menu bar consists of four links — Home, New Releases, Actor, and Type — which link to the Web pages, bellvideohome.htm, newreleases.htm, actor.htm, and type.htm, respectively. Each link is inserted in a single column (cell). The | (pipe) symbol is included in a column between each of the four links to separate them visually.

As shown in Table 4-6, the width of each column in the table is specified using the width attribute of the <td> tag. For the four cells with text links, the column widths are set so that the text fits in the cell without wrapping. For example, the column used for New Releases is set a width of 25%, while the columns used for shorter words, Home, Actor, and Type, are set to 20%, 15%, and 15%, respectively. The column widths for the cells with the | (pipe) symbols are set to 1%, because the symbol does not require much space in the menu bar. If a width of 1% is not specified for the cells with the | symbols, all cells in the table are spaced evenly, which makes the cells for the | symbol unnecessarily large.

The steps on the next page show how to create a horizontal menu bar with text links for the New Releases Web page.

To Create a Horizontal Menu Bar with Text Links

1

• If necessary, click line 16.

2

• Enter the HTML code as shown in Table 4-6 on the previous page.

3

• Press the ENTER key twice.

The HTML code is displayed (Figure 4-28).

FIGURE 4-28

The HTML code for the horizontal menu bar is complete. As shown in Figure 4-28, line 16 created a new, borderless table with seven columns that fills 60% of the window's width. Line 18 added a data cell with a text link to the bellvideohome.htm Web page, while line 20 added a text link to the newreleases.htm Web page currently under development. Lines 22 and 24 created two other test links to the actor.htm (Actor) and type.htm (Type) Web pages. Lines 19, 21, and 23 add the | (pipe) symbols to separate all of these links.

Creating a Table with Borders

Up to this point, the tables created in the Bell Video home page and New Releases Web page have been borderless. Borderless tables often are appropriate when the tables are used to position text and image elements. In other instances, such as when a table is used to structure columns and rows of information, borders are appropriate. For example, the New Releases Web page lists four columns and six rows of information about newly released movies. Figure 4-29 shows this information in a table with borders, while Figure 4-30 shows the same table without borders. As shown in these figures, using a table with borders makes the information on the New Releases Web page easier to read and provides a frame that gives the table a three-dimensional appearance.

columns and rows separated by borders

FIGURE 4-29   Table with border.

columns and rows not separated by borders

FIGURE 4-30   Borderless table.

Creating a Table with Borders and Inserting Text into Cells

Creating the table shown in Figure 4-29 on the previous page first involves creating a table with four columns and seven rows. The first row of the table is for column headings; the other rows are for data. As you have learned, heading cells differ from data cells in their appearance. Text in a heading cell appears as bold and centered, while text in a data cell appears as normal and left-aligned. Table 4-7 contains the HTML tags and text used to create the table of newly released movies on the New Releases Web page.

Table 4-7 HTML Code to Create a Table with Borders and Insert Text into Cells	
LINE	HTML TAG AND TEXT
28	` <table cols="4" border="5" width="80%">`
29	`<tr bgcolor="lightsteelblue'>`
30	`<th><font color="#993366" size="11">Titles</font></th>`
31	`<th><font color="#993366" size="+1">Type</font></th>`
32	`<th><font color="#993366" size="+1">Actor(s)</font></th>`
33	`<th><font color="#993366" size="+1">Rating</font></th>`
34	`</tr>`
35	
36	`<tr>`
37	`<td>The Lord of the Rings:`
38	` The Fellowship of the Ring</td>`
39	`<td>Fantasy</td>`
40	`<td>Ian McKellen`
41	` Elijah Wood</td>`
42	`<td>PG-13</td>`
43	`</tr>`
44	
45	`<tr>`
46	`<td>The Matrix Revolutions</td>`
47	`<td>Action</td>`
48	`<td>Keanu Reeves`
49	` Laurence Fishburne</td>`
50	`<td>R</td>`
51	`</tr>`

The following steps illustrate how to create a table with borders and insert text into heading and data cells.

To Create a Table with Borders and Insert Text

1
- **If necessary, click line 28.**

2
- **Enter the HTML code as shown in Table 4-7.**

3
- **Press the ENTER key twice.**

The HTML code is displayed (Figure 4-31).

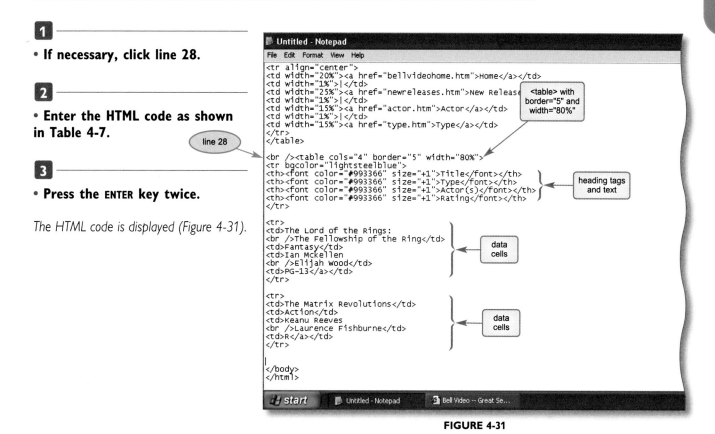

FIGURE 4-31

As shown in Figure 4-31, line 28 created a four-column table with a border that is five pixels wide. The table spans 80% of the window's width. Line 30 inserted a table header row with a light steel blue background and a large size (+1) font. Lines 31 through 33 added the three remaining headers. Lines 37 through 50 used the <td> </td> tags to create five rows with four data cells per row and then to insert text in the data cells.

Table 4-8 on the next page lists the HTML tags and text to create the remaining data cells and insert text.

Table 4-8 HTML Code to Create Additional Cells and Insert Text

53	`<tr>`
54	`<td>Mona Lisa Smile</td>`
55	`<td>Drama</td>`
56	`<td>Julia Roberts</td>`
57	`<td>PG-13</td>`
58	`</tr>`
59	
60	`<tr>`
61	`<td>Something's Gotta Give</td>`
62	`<td>Comedy</td>`
63	`<td>Jack Nicholson`
64	` Diane Keaton</td>`
65	`<td>PG-13</td>`
66	`</tr>`
67	
68	`<tr>`
69	`<td>Runaway Jury</td>`
70	`<td>Drama</td>`
71	`<td>Gene Hackman`
72	` John Cusack</td>`
73	`<td>PG-13</td>`
74	`</tr>`

As shown in Table 4-8, each row of text is defined using the <tr> and </tr> tags. Each cell of text within that row is defined using the <td> and </td> tags. In this table, each row has four data cells, so four sets of <td> </td> tags are added per row. The following steps show how to create additional cells and insert text into those cells.

To Create Additional Cells and Insert Text

1 If necessary, click line 53.

2 Enter the HTML code as shown in Table 4-8.

The HTML code is displayed (Figure 4-32).

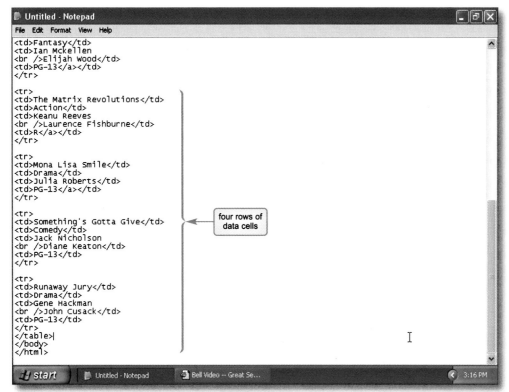

```
Untitled - Notepad
File  Edit  Format  View  Help
<td>Fantasy</td>
<td>Ian Mckellen
<br />Elijah Wood</td>
<td>PG-13</a></td>
</tr>

<tr>
<td>The Matrix Revolutions</td>
<td>Action</td>
<td>Keanu Reeves
<br />Laurence Fishburne</td>
<td>R</a></td>
</tr>

<tr>
<td>Mona Lisa Smile</td>
<td>Drama</td>
<td>Julia Roberts</td>
<td>PG-13</a></td>
</tr>

<tr>
<td>Something's Gotta Give</td>
<td>Comedy</td>
<td>Jack Nicholson
<br />Diane Keaton</td>
<td>PG-13</td>
</tr>

<tr>
<td>Runaway Jury</td>
<td>Drama</td>
<td>Gene Hackman
<br />John Cusack</td>
<td>PG-13</td>
</tr>
</table>|
</body>
</html>
```

four rows of
data cells

start   Untitled - Notepad   Bell Video -- Great Se...   3:16 PM

FIGURE 4-32

The HTML code for the table with borders is complete. Lines 53, 60, and 68 added three new rows of data cells using the <tr> (start table row) tag. Lines 58, 66, and 74 ended each row with a </tr> (end table row) tag. All of the text information was inserted into data cells between the <tr> and </tr> tags.

With the HTML code for the table with borders added, the New Releases Web page is complete. The HTML file thus should be saved and a copy should be printed as a reference.

To Save and Print an HTML File

1 With a floppy disk in drive A, click File on the menu bar and then click Save As. Type `newreleases.htm` in the File name text box.

2 If necessary, click 3½ Floppy (A:) in the Save in list. Click the Project04 folder and then click the ProjectFiles folder in the list of available folders. Click the Save button in the Save As dialog box.

3 Click File on the menu bar and then click Print on the file menu.

Notepad saves the HTML file in the Project04\ProjectFiles folder on the floppy disk in drive A using the file name, newreleases.htm. Notepad prints the HTML file (Figure 4-33 on the next page).

```
<!DOCTYPE html
    PUBLIC "-//W3C//DTD XHTML 1.0 Transitional//EN"
    "http://www.w3.org/TR/xhtml1/DTD/xhtml1-transitional.dtd">

<html>
<head>
<title>Bell Video - New Releases</title>
</head>
<body>
<table border="0" cols="1" width="10%">
<tr>
<td><img src="bellvideologo.gif" width="430" height="74" alt="Bell Video Logo" /></td>
</tr>
</table>

<br /><table border="0" cols="7" width="60%">
<tr align="center">
<td width="20%"><a href="bellvideohome.htm">Home</a></td>
<td width="1%">|</td>
<td width="25%"><a href="newreleases.htm">New Releases</a></td>
<td width="1%">|</td>
<td width="15%"><a href="actor.htm">Actor</a></td>
<td width="1%">|</td>
<td width="15%"><a href="type.htm">Type</a></td>
</tr>
</table>

<br /><table cols="4" border="5" width="80%">
<tr bgcolor="lightsteelblue">
<th><font color="#993366" size="+1">Title</font></th>
<th><font color="#993366" size="+1">Type</font></th>
<th><font color="#993366" size="+1">Actor(s)</font></th>
<th><font color="#993366" size="+1">Rating</font></th>
</tr>

<tr>
<td>The Lord of the Rings:
<br />The Fellowship of the Ring</td>
<td>Fantasy</td>
<td>Ian Mckellen
<br />Elijah Wood</td>
<td>PG-13</td>
</tr>

<tr>
<td>The Matrix Revolutions</td>
<td>Action</td>
<td>Keanu Reeves
<br />Laurence Fishburne</td>
<td>R</td>
</tr>

<tr>
<td>Mona Lisa Smile</td>
<td>Drama</td>
<td>Julia Roberts</td>
<td>PG-13</td>
</tr>

<tr>
<td>Somethingís Gotta Give</td>
<td>Comedy</td>
<td>Jack Nicholson
<br />Diane Keaton</td>
<td>PG-13</td>
</tr>

<tr>
<td>Runaway Jury</td>
<td>Drama</td>
<td>Gene Hackman
<br />John Cusack</td>
<td>PG-13</td>
</tr>
</table>

</body>
</html>
```

FIGURE 4-33

After saving and printing the HTML file, perform the following steps to view and print the Web page.

To View and Print the Web Page Using the Browser

1 Click the Internet Explorer button on the taskbar.

2 Click the New Releases link in the vertical menu bar on the Bell Video home page.

3 Click the Print button on the Standard Buttons toolbar, when the New Releases Web page is displayed.

The New Releases Web page is displayed (Figure 4-34).

FIGURE 4-34

As shown in Figure 4-34, the New Releases Web page includes three tables: a two-row, one-column borderless table used to position the logo image; a one-row, seven-column table used to create a horizontal menu bar with links to all other Web pages; and a six-row, four-column table that contains the information about newly released movies available at Bell Video.

After confirming that the Web page appears as desired, the four links in the horizontal menu bar should be tested to verify that they function as expected. The steps on the next page show how to test the links in the New Releases Web page.

To Test Links in a Web Page

1 Click the Home link in the horizontal menu bar on the New Releases Web page.

2 Click the New Releases link in the vertical menu bar on the home page to return to the New Releases Web page.

3 Click the Type link in the horizontal menu bar on the New Releases Web page.

4 Click the Actor link in the horizontal menu bar on the Type Web page.

The Actor Web page is displayed (Figure 4-35).

FIGURE 4-35

Thus far, the project has illustrated how to create the Bell Video home page and New Releases Web page. The HTML files for the other two Web pages (actor.htm and type.htm) are available in the Project04\ProjectFiles folder on the HTML Data Disk. Figure 4-35 shows the Actor Web page as saved on the HTML Data Disk. This Web page and the Type Web page both currently contain a borderless table with the logo image, a table used for a horizontal menu bar, and a table with borders used to organize text in data cells. The remaining sections in this project illustrate how to enhance the appearance of the actor.htm and type.htm Web pages using cellpadding, cellspacing, a caption, and headings that span rows and columns.

Adding Cellspacing, Cellpadding, and a Caption

The table of information on the New Releases Web page did not use the cellspacing or cellpadding attributes. The size of each data cell, therefore, automatically was set to the minimum size needed for the text inserted in the data cell.

The Actor Web page, however, should be modified to use cellspacing and cellpadding by adding the cellspacing and cellpadding attributes to the <table> tag. As shown in Table 4-2 on page HTM 142, **cellspacing** defines the number of pixels of space between cells in a table. **Cellpadding** defines the number of pixels of space within a cell. Figure 4-36 illustrates how using the <table> tag attributes cellspacing and cellpadding can affect a table's appearance.

FIGURE 4-36 Tables with cellpadding and cellspacing.

Adding Cellspacing and Cellpadding to a Table

Figure 4-37a shows how the Actor Web page stored on the HTML Data Disk looks as currently designed. Figure 4-37b shows how the Actor Web page will appear after cellspacing, cellpadding, and a caption are added.

(a) **Actor Web page before enhancements.**

(b) **Actor Web page after enhancements.**

FIGURE 4-37

The following steps show to activate Notepad and open the Actor Web page file stored on the HTML Data Disk.

To Open an HTML File

1 Click the Notepad button on the taskbar.

2 With the HTML Data Disk in drive A, click File on the menu bar and then click Open on the File menu.

3 If necessary, click the Look in box arrow and then click 3½ Floppy (A:). Click the Project04 folder and then click the ProjectFiles folder in the list of available folders.

4 If necessary, click the Files of type box arrow and then click All Files.

5 Click actor.htm in the list of files.

6 Click the Open button in the Open dialog box.

Notepad opens the file, actor.htm (Figure 4-38). The first 40 lines of the HTML code for actor.htm are displayed.

FIGURE 4-38

With the file actor.htm open, the HTML code to add cellspacing and cellpadding can be added. The steps on the next page show how to add cellspacing and cellpadding to a table.

To Add Cellspacing and Cellpadding to a Table

1

• **Click immediately to the right of the 5 in border="5" in line 28 and then press the SPACEBAR.**

2

• **Type** cellspacing="2" cellpadding="5" **as the attributes.**

The HTML code is displayed (Figure 4-39).

FIGURE 4-39

Adding the <table> tag attributes, cellspacing="2" and cellpadding="5", enhances the table by adding two pixels of space between cells and five pixels of space within the cells in the table. As shown in Figure 4-37b on page HTM 170, adding space between and within cells makes the table appear less cluttered and easier to read.

Adding a Table Caption

As you have learned, a caption can help clarify the purpose of a table. For some tables, such as the table used to position images and the tables used to create menu bars, captions are not appropriate. Tables used to structure columns and rows of information, such as the Actor table, can benefit from having a caption to clarify the contents of the table. A table caption is added to a table using code such as:

```
<caption align="bottom"><em>Listing of movies by actor</em></caption>
```

where the <caption> </caption> tags enclose the caption text. This caption also uses the <em> </em> tags to italicize the caption text. The align attribute determines the placement of the caption. A caption can be placed above or below the table using the align="above" or align="bottom" attributes, respectively.

The following steps show how to add a caption below the Actor table.

To Add a Table Caption

1

• **Highlight the text <!--Insert caption here --> on line 69.**

2

• **Type** `<caption align= "bottom"><em>Listing of movies by actor</em> </caption>` **as the tag.**

The HTML code is displayed (Figure 4-40).

```
 actor - Notepad
File  Edit  Format  View  Help
<td>Gladiator</td>
<td>Drama</td>
</tr>

<tr>
<td>Russell Crowe</td>
<td>A Beautiful Mind</td>
<td>Drama</td>
</tr>

<tr>
<td>Diane Keaton</td>
<td>Something's Gotta Give</td>
<td>Comedy</td>
</tr>

<tr>
<td>Julia Roberts</td>
<td>Pretty Woman</td>
<td>Romance</td>
</tr>

<tr>
<td>Julia Roberts</td>
<td>Mona Lisa Smile</td>
<td>Drama</td>
</tr>

<tr>
<td>Gene Wilder</td>
<td>Young Frankenstein</td>
<td>Comedy</td>
</tr>
<caption align="bottom"><em>Listing of movies by actor</em></caption>|
</table>

</body>
</html>
```

line 69

table caption

 start | actor - Notepad | Bell Video - Actor - Mi...

FIGURE 4-40

With the HTML code for the table caption added, the Actor Web page is complete. The HTML file thus should be saved and a copy should be printed as a reference. After saving and printing the HTML file, the Web page should be viewed and also printed as a reference.

To Save and Print the HTML File and View and Print the Web Page

1 With the floppy disk in drive A, click File on the menu bar and then click Save.

2 Click File on the menu bar and then click Print.

3 Click the Internet Explorer button on the taskbar.

4 Click the Refresh button on the Standard Buttons toolbar.

5 Click the Print button on the Standard Buttons toolbar.

Notepad saves the updated HTML file in the Project04\ProjectFiles folder on the floppy disk in drive A using the file name, actor.htm. The Actor Web page is displayed (Figure 4-41 on the next page). The HTML file and Web page are printed.

FIGURE 4-41

Spanning Rows and Columns

Spanning rows and columns is a technique used frequently to create a heading that goes across, or spans, rows or columns. As shown in Table 4-2 on page HTM 146, the **rowspan attribute** of the <th> or <td> tag sets the number of rows spanned by a cell, while the **colspan attribute** of the <th> or <td> tag sets the number of columns spanned by a cell. Figure 4-9 on page HTM 140 shows an example of a table that uses the rowspan and colspan attributes.

Figure 4-42 shows the Type Web page as saved on the HTML Data Disk. The table in this Web page is incomplete because the Web page visitor cannot tell what the table means without headings of any kind. Figure 4-43 shows how the Type Web page will appear after headings that span rows and columns are added.

no headings

FIGURE 4-42 Type Web page before enhancements.

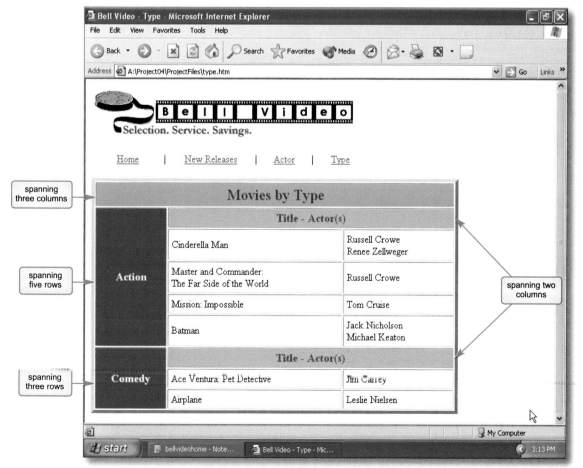

spanning three columns

spanning five rows

spanning two columns

spanning three rows

FIGURE 4-43 Type Web page after enhancements.

The first step when deciding to span rows or columns is to sketch the table design on a piece of paper, as shown in Figure 4-44. The table organizes movies by type and thus should have a main heading, Movies by Type. Two different types of movies are represented by the information in the rows: Action and Comedy. The columns in the table also require subheadings to indicate what information is included about each movie.

Movies by Type		
Action	Title - Actor(s)	
	Cinderella Man	Russell Crowe Renee Zellweger
	Master and Commander: The Far Side of the World	Russell Crowe
	Mission: Impossible	Tom Cruise
	Batman	Jack Nicholson Michael Keaton
Comedy	Title - Actor(s)	
	Ace Ventura: Pet Detective	Jim Carrey
	Airplane	Leslie Nielsen

FIGURE 4-44

After defining the main sections of a table, you must determine how many rows or columns each heading should span. For example, the title heading for the table should span all three table columns. The heading for the first main section (Action) should span four rows, while the heading for the second section (Comedy) should span two rows. The row headings, Title - Actor(s), should span two columns.

The following steps show how to open the file, type.htm, from the HTML Data Disk and then add rowspan and colspan attributes to create table headings.

To Open an HTML File

1 Click the Notepad button on the taskbar.

2 With the HTML Data Disk in drive A, click File on the menu bar and then click Open on the File menu.

3 If necessary, click the Look in box arrow and then click 3½ Floppy (A:). Click the Project04 folder and then click the ProjectFiles folder in the list of available folders.

4 If necessary, click the Files of type box arrow, click All Files, and then double-click type.htm in the list of files.

Notepad displays the type.htm file.

Spanning the Main Heading across All Columns

As shown in Figure 4-43 on page HTM 175, the main heading for the table is in a new row, above the first row of text that currently is in the table. The main heading spans across both of the existing columns, as well as the new column that is created on the left. The main heading has one line — Movies by Type.

To Span the Main Heading across All Columns

1

• **Highlight the <!--Insert Movies by Type colspan here --> text on line 29. Type** <tr> **and then press the ENTER key.**

2

• **Type** <th colspan="3" bgcolor= "lightsteelblue"> **and then press the ENTER key.**

FIGURE 4-45

3

• **Type** <font color="#993366" face="chaucer" size="+2">Movies by Type</font> **and then press the ENTER key.**

4

• **Type** </th> **and then press the ENTER key.**

5

• **Type** </tr> **as the end table row tag.**

The HTML code is displayed (Figure 4-45).

Entering the <tr> tag in Step 1 created a new row. The <th> tag created a heading cell that spans three columns of the table and uses a light steel blue background color. The code entered in Step 3 changed the font to Chaucer using a larger (+2) size font. Finally, Steps 4 and 5 ended the heading cell and the row. If the HTML file was saved and viewed it in a browser at this point, the table would appear as shown in Figure 4-46.

FIGURE 4-46

Creating Additional Headings that Span Rows and Columns

The next step is to create two columns that span five and three rows in the body of the table, respectively. Although only six rows contain cast member names, the HTML code for the two columns must account for the two additional header rows for another heading (Title - Actor(s)), which will be added later. Table 4-9 lists the HTML code required to create a heading column that spans five rows and the first row heading that spans two columns.

Table 4-9 HTML Code for Additional Headings

34	`<tr bgcolor="#ffffff">`
35	`<th rowspan="5" width="20%" bgcolor="#336699">`
36	`<font color="#ffffff" size=+1>Action</font>`
37	`</th>`
38	`<th colspan="2" bgcolor="thistle">`
39	`<font color="#336699" size="+1">Title - Actor(s)</font>`
40	`</th>`
41	`</tr>`

The following steps illustrate how to enter HTML code to create a heading column that spans five rows and the first row heading that spans two columns.

To Create Headings that Span Rows and Columns

1

• **Highlight <!--Insert Action rowspan here --> text on line 34.**

2

• **Enter the HTML code as shown in Table 4-9.**

The HTML code is displayed (Figure 4-47.)

FIGURE 4-47

Line 34 created a new table row and line 35 added a table header that spans five rows of the table to identify Action movies listed in the table rows. Line 36 added the heading text, Action, in a white, larger (+1) size font. Line 38 created a new table header within the row and set it to span two table columns. Line 39 added the heading text, Title - Actor(s), in a light blue, larger (+1) size font. If the HTML file was saved and viewed in a browser at this point, the table would appear as shown in Figure 4-48 on the next page.

FIGURE 4-48

To Create the Second Heading that Spans Rows

1 Highlight the **<!--Insert Comedy rowspan here -->** text on line 66 and then press the DELETE key.

2 Type **<tr>** and then press the ENTER key.

3 Type **<th rowspan="4" bgcolor="#336699">** and then press the ENTER key.

4 Type **<font color="#ffffff" size="+1">Comedy</font>** and then press the ENTER key.

5 Type **</th>** as the tag.

The HTML code is displayed (Figure 4-49).

FIGURE 4-49

The previous steps added another table header that spans rows, to identify Comedy movies listed in the table rows. This second table header uses the same formatting as the Action table header added in previous steps.

The following steps illustrate how to enter HTML code to add the remaining heading that spans several columns.

To Create the Second Heading that Spans Columns

1 Highlight the **<!--Insert Title - Actor(s) colspan here -->** text on line 70.

2 Type **<th colspan="2" bgcolor="thistle">** and then press the ENTER key.

3 Type **<font color="#336699" size="+1">Title - Actor(s)</font>** and then press the ENTER key.

4 Type **</th>** and then press the ENTER key.

5 Type **</tr>** and then press the ENTER key.

The HTML code is displayed (Figure 4-50 on the next page).

In Steps 1 and 2, you added another heading, Title - Actor(s), that spans two columns. This table header uses the same formatting as the Title - Actor(s) header added in previous steps.

With the HTML code for the table headers added, the Type Web page is complete. The HTML file thus should be saved and a copy should be printed as a reference. After saving and printing the HTML file, the Web page should be viewed and also printed as a reference.

FIGURE 4-50

To Save and Print the HTML File and View and Print the Web Page

1 With the HTML Data Disk in drive A, click File on the menu bar and then click Save.

2 Click File on the menu bar and then click Print.

3 Click the Internet Explorer button on the taskbar.

4 Click the Refresh button on the Standard Buttons toolbar.

5 Click the Print button on the Standard Buttons toolbar.

Notepad saves the updated HTML file in the Project04\ProjectFiles folder on the floppy disk in drive A using the file name, type.htm. The Type Web page is displayed (Figure 4-51). The HTML file and Web page are printed.

All four Web pages for the Bell Video Web site now are complete. In this project, two new Web pages (bellvideohome.htm and newreleases.htm) were created and two existing Web pages (actor.htm and type.htm) were enhanced by adding new formatting to existing tables.

With the Type page displayed in the browser, click each of the links in the page to verify that each link connects to the appropriate Web page or link target. If possible, view all of the Web pages in more than one browser type or version to ensure that the Web pages display correctly in different browsers.

After completing the project, quit Notepad and the browser. The following steps show how to quit Notepad and a browser.

FIGURE 4-51

To Quit Notepad and a Browser

1 Click the Close button on the browser title bar.

2 Click the Close button on the Notepad window title bar.

Both the browser and Notepad windows close, and the Windows desktop is displayed.

Project Summary

In this project, you used Notepad to create and edit four HTML files and add links from each page to all three others. You learned to define table elements and the steps used to plan, design, and code a table. Using various table tags and attributes, you learned to create both bordered and borderless tables to organize images and text. You learned to use tables to create vertical and horizontal menu bars of text links, so users can navigate between all four pages in the Web site. Additionally, you learned to enhance a table format by adding background color to rows and cells, setting the spacing between and within cells using the cellspacing and cellpadding attributes, and adding a table caption. Finally, you learned how to create table headers that span rows and columns and help provide information about the data in a table.

What You Should Know

Having completed this project, you should be able to perform the tasks listed below. The tasks are listed in the same order they were presented in this project.

1. Start Notepad (HTM 143)
2. Enter HTML Tags to Define the Web Page Structure (HTM 144)
3. Create a Borderless Table to Position Images (HTM 147)
4. Insert Images in a Table (HTM 147)
5. Create a Vertical Menu Bar with Text Links (HTM 150)
6. Add Text to a Table Cell (HTM 152)
7. Save and Print the HTML File (HTM 153)
8. View and Print a Web Page (HTM 154)
9. Copy and Paste HTML Code to a New File (HTM 156)
10. Change the Title (HTM 157)
11. Delete an Image (HTM 158)
12. Create a Horizontal Menu Bar with Text Links (HTM 160)
13. Create a Table with Borders and Insert Text (HTM 163)
14. Create Additional Cells and Insert Text (HTM 164)
15. Save and Print an HTML File (HTM 165)
16. View and Print the Web Page Using the Browser (HTM 167)
17. Test Links in a Web Page (HTM 168)
18. Open an HTML File (HTM 171, HTM 177)
19. Add Cellspacing and Cellpadding to a Table (HTM 172)
20. Add a Table Caption (HTM 173)
21. Save and Print the HTML File and View and Print the Web Page (HTM 173, HTM 182)
22. Span the Main Heading across All Columns (HTM 177)
23. Create Headings that Span Rows and Columns (HTM 179)
24. Create the Second Heading that Spans Rows (HTM 180)
25. Create the Second Heading that Spans Columns (HTM 181)
26. Quit Notepad and a Browser (HTM 183)

Learn It Online

Instructions: To complete the Learn It Online exercises, start your browser, click the Address bar, and then enter the Web address scsite.com/html3e/learn. When the HTML Learn It Online page is displayed, follow the instructions in the exercises below. Each exercise has instructions for printing your results, either for your own records or for submission to your instructor.

1 Project Reinforcement TF, MC, and SA

Below HTML Project 4, click the Project Reinforcement link. Print the quiz by clicking Print on the File menu for each page. Answer each question.

2 Flash Cards

Below HTML Project 4, click the Flash Cards link and read the instructions. Type 20 (or a number specified by your instructor) in the Number of playing cards text box, type your name in the Enter your Name text box, and then click the Flip Card button. When the flash card is displayed, read the question and then click the ANSWER box arrow to select an answer. Flip through Flash Cards. If your score is 15 (75%) correct or greater, click Print on the File menu to print your results. If your score is less than 15 (75%) correct, then redo this exercise by clicking the Replay button.

3 Practice Test

Below HTML Project 4, click the Practice Test link. Answer each question, enter your first and last name at the bottom of the page, and then click the Grade Test button. When the graded practice test is displayed on your screen, click Print on the File menu to print a hard copy. Continue to take practice tests until you score 80% or better.

4 Who Wants To Be a Computer Genius?

Below HTML Project 4, click the Computer Genius link. Read the instructions, enter your first and last name at the bottom of the page, and then click the PLAY button. When your score is displayed, click the PRINT RESULTS link to print a hard copy.

5 Wheel of Terms

Below HTML Project 4, click the Wheel of Terms link. Read the instructions, and then enter your first and last name and your school name. Click the PLAY button. When your score is displayed, right-click the score and then click Print on the shortcut menu to print a hard copy.

6 Crossword Puzzle Challenge

Below HTML Project 4, click the Crossword Puzzle Challenge link. Read the instructions, and then enter your first and last name. Click the SUBMIT button. Work the crossword puzzle. When you are finished, click the Submit button. When the crossword puzzle is redisplayed, click the Print Puzzle button to print a hard copy.

7 Tips and Tricks

Below HTML Project 4, click the Tips and Tricks link. Click a topic that pertains to Project 4. Right-click the information and then click Print on the shortcut menu. Construct a brief example of what the information relates to in HTML to confirm you understand how to use the tip or trick.

8 Newsgroups

Below HTML Project 4, click the Newsgroups link. Click a topic that pertains to Project 4. Print three comments.

9 Expanding Your Horizons

Below HTML Project 4, click the Expanding Your Horizons link. Click a topic that pertains to Project 4. Print the information. Construct a brief example of what the information relates to in HTML to confirm you understand the contents of the article.

10 Search Sleuth

Below HTML Project 4, click the Search Sleuth link. To search for a term that pertains to this project, select a term below the Project 4 title and then use the Google search engine at google.com (or any major search engine) to display and print two Web pages that present information on the term.

11 Online Help I

Below HTML Project 4, click the Online Help I link. Follow the instructions on the page to access Web pages that provide additional help on project topics. Hand in any printed information to your instructor.

12 Online Help II

Below HTML Project 4, click the Online Help II link. Follow the instructions on the page to access Web pages that provide additional help on project topics. Hand in any printed information to your instructor.

Apply Your Knowledge

1 Editing the Apply Your Knowledge Web Page

Instructions: Start Notepad. Open the file, apply4-1.htm, from the Project04\AYK folder on the HTML Data Disk. If you do not have the HTML Data Disk, see the inside back cover for instructions or see your instructor. The apply4-1.htm file is a partially completed HTML file that contains some errors. Figure 4-52 shows the Apply Your Knowledge Web page as it should display in the browser after the errors are corrected. Perform the following steps using a computer.

FIGURE 4-52

The table shown in the figure:

PROJECT MANAGEMENT Responsibility Chart					
	J. P. Walker	Mary Davids	Dion El-Sharif	Lashon Tyler	Azher Alia
Scope Management	X		X	X	
Time Management			X	X	X
Cost Management	X	X			
Quality Management	X			X	
Human Resource Management		X			X
Risk Management	X			X	X
Communication Management		X	X		

1. Enter the URL, a:\Project04\AYK\apply4-1.htm, to view the Web page in your browser.
2. Examine the HTML file and its appearance as a Web page in the browser.
3. Correct the HTML errors, making the Web page look similar to the Web page shown in Figure 4-52.
4. Add any HTML code necessary for additional features shown in the Web page in Figure 4-52.
5. Save the revised file in the Project04\AYK folder on the HTML Data Disk using the file name, apply4-1solution.htm.
6. Print the revised HTML file.
7. Enter the URL, a:\Project04\AYK\apply4-1solution.htm, to view the Web page in your browser.
8. Print the Web page.
9. Write your name on both printouts and hand them in to your instructor.

1 Creating a Table with Multiple Images

Problem: Bell Video wants to review other customer service award logos for potential use on the home page and compare them with the image currently being used, csexcellence.gif. You have been asked to create a Web page that shows the four logo samples, similar to the one shown in Figure 4-53.

FIGURE 4-53

Instructions: Start Notepad. Perform the following steps using a computer.

1. Start a new HTML file with the title [your name] lab4-1 in the main heading section.
2. Insert the text shown in the top line of the Web page.
3. Add a centered borderless table with two columns and two rows and cellpadding of 25.
3. Insert the image, csexcellence.gif, in the first column of the first row.
4. Add the second image, csexcellence_v1.gif, to that same row in a second column.
5. Start a new row and add the images, csexcellence_v2.gif and csexcellence_v3.gif.
6. Save the HTML file in the Project04\IntheLab folder on the HTML Data Disk using the file name, lab4-1solution.htm.
8. Print the lab4-1solution.htm file.
9. Open the file, lab4-1solution.htm, in your browser to view it as a Web page.
10. Print the Web page.
11. Write your name on the printouts and hand them in to your instructor.

2 Creating Two Borderless Tables

Problem: Your manager at Mirimar Web Group, L.L.C. has asked you to create two Web pages, similar to the ones shown in Figures 4-54a and 4-54b. The first Web page is a home page that presents information about Mirimar Web Group, L.L.C., together with two links. The Samples link in the first page will be linked to the Bell Video home page created in Project 4. The second Web page lists the pricing structure Mirimar charges for various Web development phases.

Instructions: Start Notepad. Perform the following steps using a computer.

1. Start a new HTML file with the title [your name] lab4-2a in the main heading section.
2. Create a 50% wide, one-row, two-column borderless table with the image, computer.gif, in the left-hand data cell and the image, webgrouplogo.gif, in the right-hand data cell.
3. Create a second one-row, two-column borderless table. Make the first column 20% wide with a background color of yellow and then add two links to the column: Pricing (lab4-2bsolution.htm) and Samples (ProjectFiles\bellvideohome.htm). Make the second column 70% wide and include the text and an e-mail link as shown in Figure 4-54a.
4. Save the HTML file using the file name, lab4-2asolution.htm, in the Project04\IntheLab folder on the HTML Data Disk. Print the HTML file.
5. Start a new HTML file with the title [your name] lab4-2b in the main heading section.
6. Create a five-row, two-column table with a five-pixel border, cellpadding of 15, and cellspacing of 5. Use yellow for the background color of the top row and the color #e0e0e0 for all other rows.
7. Span the first heading across both columns, as shown in Figure 4-54b.
8. Enter the headings, Service and Hourly Rate, and additional information in the appropriate table cells, as shown in Figure 4-54b.
9. Save the HTML file in the Project04\IntheLab folder on the HTML Data Disk using the file name, lab4-2bsolution.htm. Print the HTML file.
10. Open the file, lab4-2asolution.htm, in your browser and test the Pricing link to verify it links to the lab4-2bsolution.htm Web page.
11. Print both Web pages.
12. Write your name on all printouts and hand them in to your instructor.

(a)

(b)

FIGURE 4-54

In the Lab

3 Creating Linked Schedules

Problem: You want to create two Web pages similar to the ones shown in Figures 4-55a and 4-55b, which list your school and work schedule. The Web pages will use tables with headings that span several rows and columns to organize the information and will include links from one page to the other.

Instructions: Start Notepad. Perform the following steps using a computer.

1. Start two new HTML files with the titles [your name] lab4-3a and [your name] lab4-3b, respectively, in the main heading section.
2. In the lab4-3a file (School), create a borderless table with a menu bar (Figures 4-55a). In the lab 4-3b file (Work), create a one-pixel-bordered table with a menu bar (Figures 4-55b)
3. Include the headings and data cells as shown in both pages, with valid information in the data cells.
4. Add background colors for cells, as you see fit.
5. Save the HTML files in the Project04\IntheLab folder on the HTML Data Disk using the file names lab4-3asolution.htm and lab4-3bsolution.htm, respectively. Print the HTML files.
7. Open the file, lab4-3asolution.htm, in your browser and test the Work link to verify it links to the lab4-3bsolution.htm Web page. Test the School link to verify it links to the lab4-3asolution.htm Web page. Print both Web pages from your browser.
8. Write your name on all printouts and hand them in to your instructor.

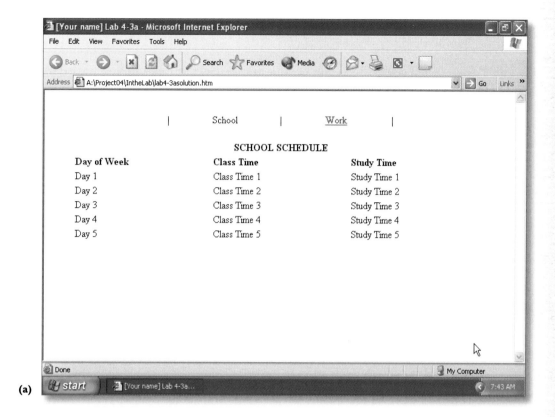

(a)

(b)

FIGURE 4-55

Cases and Places

The difficulty of these case studies varies:
■ are the least difficult and ■■ are the most difficult. The last exercise is a group exercise.

1 ■ In the Lab 1 you created a Web page that includes three new customer service award logos that could be used on the Bell Video home page. After seeing the new logos, the management staff at Bell Video has asked you to modify the Bell Video home page to test the new logos and determine if one of them is a better fit for the Web page. They also have asked you to insert a logo image on the three other Bell Video Web pages, so they can review how that would look. After modifying the Bell Video Web pages, have other students evaluate the new pages, comparing them with what was created in Project 4.

2 ■■ Browse the Web to find three Web pages that contain borderless tables and three Web pages that contain tables with borders. To verify, you can check the Web page source code from within the browser. Print all six pages and indicate if these are appropriate uses of each type of table and why. Next, find three Web pages that do not use tables currently but that should, in your opinion. Determine how these pages might display their content more effectively with the use of tables. Print those three pages and sketch Web page designs that incorporate tables.

3 ■■ Last week, you and the owner of Trailways Bus Lines sketched out a basic table format to use on the Updated Prices Web page of the Trailways Bus Lines Web site. As you begin to build the Web page, you start thinking about other table attributes that could make the Web pages look even better. Create a Web page with a basic five-row, two-column table with a one-pixel border. Review the additional table attributes listed in Appendix A, including the rules attribute. Find information on those attributes on other Web sites, including the W3C Web site (www.w3.org). Modify the basic table in the Updated Prices Web page to incorporate at least four of these attributes.

4 ■■ Several developers on your Web design team at Solid Graphics have asked if you can create a Web page with a table listing the six-digit number codes for browser-safe colors. Browse the Web to find Web pages with browser-safe color charts that are created using tables. To verify, you can check the Web page source code from within the browser. Using these Web pages and Figure 2-27 on page HTM 55 as a reference, create a Web page with a table that shows at least twelve browser-safe colors. For each cell, include the six-digit number code as the text and set the background color of that cell to the same six-digit number code.

5 ■■ **Working Together** Yakima Web Design recently has been hired to build a new Web site for a local coffee shop. Your team is working creating a basic four-page Web site to share with the owners for their input. On the home page, include a menu of items (Coffees, Teas, Bakery Items) and link those items to subsequent Web pages with more detailed information about each topic. On each linked Web page, use a table to organize lists of information related to each topic (Coffees, Teas, Bakery Items). Format each table slightly differently to demonstrate topics learned in this project, such as the use of the cellspacing and cellpadding attributes, the rowspan and colspan attributes, captions, background colors, and so on.

Appendix A

HTML Quick Reference

HTML Tags and Attributes

HTML is the original language used for publishing hypertext on the World Wide Web. It is a non-proprietary format based on Standard Generalized Markup Language (SGML). HTML documents can be created with a wide variety of tools, from simple plain text editors, such as Notepad, to sophisticated WYSIWYG authoring tools, such as FrontPage. HTML uses tags such as <h1> and <p> to structure text into headings, paragraphs, lists, hypertext links, and so on.

Many HTML tags have attributes that can be defined in different ways to alter the look of the Web page even more. Table A-1 lists HTML tags and their associated attributes. The list provides a brief description of each tag and its attributes. The default value for each attribute is indicated by bold text. For a comprehensive list, more thorough descriptions, and examples of all HTML tags, visit the World Wide Web Consortium Web site at www.w3.org.

As the World Wide Web Consortium updates the current HTML specifications, HTML tags constantly are being added to, deleted, and replaced by newer tags. In this list, deprecated elements — that is, tags that can be replaced with newer elements — are indicated with an asterisk. Deprecated elements still are available for use, and most browsers still support them. Obsolete elements are elements that no longer are in use or supported by common browsers. This appendix does not list obsolete elements.

Table A-1 HTML Tags and Attributes

HTML TAG AND ATTRIBUTES	DESCRIPTION
<a>....</a>	Anchor; creates a hyperlink or fragment identifier
charset=*character set*	Specifies the character encoding of the linked resource
href=*url*	Hyperlink reference that specifies the target URL
name=*text*	Specifies a name for enclosed text, allowing it to be the target of a hyperlink
rel=*relationship*	Indicates the relationship going from the current page to the target
rev=*relationship*	Indicates the relationship going from the target to the current page
target=*name*	Defines the name of the window or frame in which the linked resource will display
<address>....</address>	Used for information such as authorship, e-mail addresses, or addresses; enclosed text displays italicized and indented in some browsers
No attributes	
<area>....</area>	Creates a clickable area, or hotspot, on a client-side imagemap
coords=*value1, value2*	Specifies the coordinates that define the edges of the hotspot; a comma-delimited list of values
href=*url*	Hyperlink reference that specifies the target URL
nohref	Indicates that no link is associated with the area
shape=*shape*	Identifies the shape of the area (poly, rect)
target=*name*	Defines the name of the window or frame in which the linked resource will display
....	Specifies text to display in bold
No attributes	
<base />	Identifies the base in all relative URLs in the document
href=*url*	Specifies the absolute URL used to resolve all relative URLs in the document
target=*name*	Defines the name for the default window or frame in which the hyperlinked pages display
<big>....</big>	Increases the size of the enclosed text to a type size bigger than the surrounding text; exact display size depends on the browser and default font
No attributes	
<blockquote>....</blockquote>	Sets enclosed text to display as a quotation, indented on the right and left
No attributes	
<body>....</body>	Defines the start and end of a Web page
alink=*color*	Defines the color of an active link
background=*url*	Identifies the image to be used as a background
bgcolor=*color*	Sets the document's background color
link=*color*	Defines the color of links not yet visited
vlink=*color*	Defines the color of visited links
<bold>....</bold>	Sets enclosed text to display in bold
No attributes	

Table A-1 HTML Tags and Attributes

HTML TAG AND ATTRIBUTES	DESCRIPTION
\<br /\>	Inserts a line break
clear=*margin*	Sets the next line to start in a spot where the requested margin is clear (left, right, all, none); used to stop text wrap
\<caption\>....\</caption\>	Creates a caption for a table
align=*position*	Sets caption position (top, bottom, left, right)
\<center\>....\</center\> *	Centers the enclosed text horizontally on the page
No attributes	
\<cite\>....\</cite\>	Indicates that the enclosed text is a citation; text usually displays in italics
No attributes	
\<code\>....\</code\>	Indicates that the enclosed text is a code sample from a program; text usually displays in fixed width font such as Courier
No attributes	
\<col\>....\</col\>	Organizes columns in a table into column groups to share attribute values
align=*position*	Sets horizontal alignment of text within the column (char, center, top, bottom, left, right)
span=*value*	Sets the number of columns that span the \<col\> element
valign=*position*	Specifies vertical alignment of text within the column (top, middle, bottom)
width=*value*	Sets the width of each column in the column group
\<colgroup\>....\</colgroup\>	Encloses a group of \<col\> tags and groups the columns to set properties
align=*position*	Specifies horizontal alignment of text within the column (char, center, top, bottom, left, right)
char=*character*	Specifies a character on which to align column values (e.g., a period is used to align monetary values)
charoff=*value*	Specifies a number of characters to offset data aligned with the character specified in the char property
span=*number*	Sets the number of columns the \<col\> element spans
valign=*position*	Specifies vertical alignment of text within the column (top, middle, bottom)
width=*value*	Sets the width of each column spanned by the colgroup statement
\<dd\>....\</dd\>	Indicates that the enclosed text is a definition in the definition list
No attributes	
\<div\>....\</div\>	Defines block-level structure or division in the HTML document
align=*position*	Specifies alignment of the content block (center, left, right)
class=*name*	Assigns the class name to each class of divisions
id=*name*	Assigns a unique name to a specific content block
\<dl\>....\</dl\>	Creates a definition list
No attributes	
\<dt\>....\</dt\>	Indicates that the enclosed text is a term in definition list
No attributes	

Table A-1 HTML Tags and Attributes (continued)

HTML TAG AND ATTRIBUTES	DESCRIPTION
\<em\>....\</em\>	Indicates that the enclosed text should be emphasized; usually displays in italics
No attributes	
\<fieldset\>....\</fieldset\>	Groups related form controls and labels
align=*position*	Specifies alignment of a legend as related to the fieldset (top, bottom, middle, left, right)
\<font\>....\</font\> *	Defines the appearance of enclosed text
size=*value*	Sets the font size in absolute terms (1 through 7) or as a relative value (e.g., +2)
color=*color*	Sets the font color; can be a hexadecimal value (#rrggbb) or a word for a predefined color value (e.g., navy)
face=*list*	Identifies the font face; multiple entries should be separated by commas
point-size=*value*	Sets the point size of text for downloaded fonts
weight=*value*	Sets the weight of the font, ranging from 100 (lightest) to 900 (heaviest)
\<form\>....\</form\>	Marks the start and end of a Web page form
action=*url*	Specifies the URL of the application that will process the form; required attribute
enctype=*encoding*	Specifies how the form element values will be encoded
method=*method*	Specifies the method used to pass form parameters (data) to the server
target=*text*	Specifies the frame or window that displays the form's results
\<frame\>....\</frame\>	Delimits a frame within a frameset
frameborder=*option*	Specifies whether the frame border displays (yes, no)
marginheight=*value*	Adds *n* pixels of space above and below the frame contents
marginwidth=*value*	Adds *n* pixels of space to the left and the right of the frame contents
name=*text*	Specifies the name of the frame
noresize	Prevents the user from resizing the frame
scrolling=*option*	Defines the URL of the source document that is displayed in the frame
src=*url*	Adds scroll bars or not – always (yes), never (no), or add when needed (**auto**)
\<frameset\>....\</frameset\>	Defines a collection of frames in a frameset
cols=*value1, value2,...*	Defines the number and width of frames within a frameset
rows= *value1, value2,...*	Defines the number and height of frames within a frameset
frameborder=*option*	Specifies whether the frame border displays (yes, no)
\<hn\>....\</hn\>	Defines a header level *n*, ranging from the largest (h1) to the smallest (h6)
align=*position*	Specifies the header alignment (**left**, center, right)
\<head\>....\</head\>	Delimits the start and end of the HTML document's head
No attributes	
\<hr /\>	Inserts a horizontal rule
align=*type*	Specifies the alignment of the horizontal rule (left, **center**, right)
noshade	Specifies to not use 3D shading and to round the ends of the rule
size=*value*	Sets the thickness of the rule to a value in pixels
width=*value or %*	Sets the width of the rule to a value in pixels or a percentage of the page width; percentage is preferred

Table A-1 HTML Tags and Attributes

HTML TAG AND ATTRIBUTES	DESCRIPTION
<html>....</html>	Indicates the start and the end of the HTML document
version=*data*	Indicates the HTML version used; not usually used
<i>....</i>	Sets enclosed text to display in italics
No attributes	
<iframe>....</iframe>	Creates an inline frame, also called a floating frame or subwindow, within an HTML document
align=*position*	Aligns the frame with respect to context (top, middle, **bottom**, left, right)
frameborder=*option*	Specifies whether a frame border displays (1=yes; 0=no)
height=*value*	Sets the frame height to a value in pixels
marginheight=*value*	Sets the margin between the contents of the frame and its top and bottom borders to a value in pixels
marginwidth=*value*	Sets the margin between the contents of the frame and its left and right borders to value in pixels
name=*text*	Assigns a name to the current frame
noresize	Prevents the user from resizing the frame
src=*url*	Defines the URL of the source document that is displayed in the frame
width=*value*	Sets the frame width to a value in pixels
scrolling=*option*	Adds scroll bars or not – always (yes), never (no), or add when needed (**auto**)
<img>....</img>	Inserts an image into the current Web page
align=*type*	Defines image alignment in relation to the text or the page margin (top, middle, bottom, right, left)
alt=*text*	Provides a text description of an image if the browser cannot display the image; always should be used
border=*value*	Sets the thickness of the border around the image to a value in pixels; default size is 3
height=*value*	Sets the height of the image to a value in pixels; always should be used
src=*url*	Specifies the URL of the image to be displayed; required
usemap=*url*	Specifies the map of coordinates and links that defines the href within this image
width=*value*	Sets the width of the image to a value in pixels; always should be used
<input>....</input>	Defines controls used in forms
alt=*text*	Provides a short description of the control or image button; for browsers that do not support inline images
checked	Sets radio buttons and check boxes to the checked state
disabled	Disables the control
maxlength=*value*	Sets a value for the maximum number of characters allowed as input for a text or password control
name=*text*	Assigns a name to the control
readonly	Prevents changes to the control
size=*value*	Sets the initial size of the control to a value in characters
src=*url*	Identifies the location of the image if the control is set to an image

Table A-1 HTML Tags and Attributes (continued)

HTML TAG AND ATTRIBUTES	DESCRIPTION
\<input\>....\</input\> *(continued)*	
tabindex=*value*	Specifies the tab order between elements in the form, with 1 as the first element
type=*type*	Defines the type of control (**text**, password, checkbox, radio, submit, reset, file, hidden, image, button)
usemap=*url*	Associates an imagemap as defined by the \<map\> element
value=*data*	Sets the initial value of the control
\<ins\>....\</ins\>	Identifies and displays text as having been inserted in the document in relation to a previous version
cite=*url*	Specifies the URL of a document that has more information on the inserted text
datetime=*datetime*	Date and time of a change
\<kbd\>....\</kbd\>	Sets enclosed text to display as keyboard-like input
No attributes	
\<label\>....\</label\>	Creates a label for a form control
for=*data*	Indicates the name or ID of the element to which the label is applied
\<legend\>....\</legend\>	Assigns a caption to a fieldset element, as defined by the \<fieldset\> tags
No attributes	
\<li\>....\</li\>	Defines the enclosed text as a list item in a list
value=*value1*	Inserts or restarts counting with value1
\<link\>....\</link\>	Establishes a link between the HTML document and another document, such as an external style sheet
charset=*character set*	Specifies the character encoding of the linked resource
href=*url*	Defines the URL of the linked document
name=*text*	Names the current anchor so that it can be the destination to other links
rel=*relationship*	Indicates the relationship going from the current page to the target
rev=*relationship*	Indicates the relationship going from the target to the current page
target=*name*	Defines the name of the frame into which the linked resource will display
type=*mime-type*	Indicates the data or media type of the linked document (e.g., text/css for linked style sheets)
\<map\>....\</map\>	Specifies a client-side imagemap; must enclose \<area\> tags
name=*text*	Assigns a name to the imagemap
\<meta /\>	Provides additional data (metadata) about an HTML document
content=*text*	Specifies the value for the \<meta\> information; required
http-equiv=*text*	Specifies the HTTP-equivalent name for metadata; tells the server to include that name and content in the HTTP header when the HTML document is sent to the client
name=*text*	Assigns a name to metadata
scheme=*text*	Provides additional context for interpreting the information in the content attribute

Table A-1 HTML Tags and Attributes

HTML TAG AND ATTRIBUTES	DESCRIPTION
<noframes>....</noframes>	Defines content to be displayed in browsers that do not support frames; very important to include
No attributes	
<object>....</object>	Includes an external object in the HTML document such as an image, a Java applet, or other external object, not well-supported by most browsers
archive=*url*	Specifies the URL of the archive containing classes and other resources that will be preloaded for use by the object
classid=*url*	Specifies the URL of the embedded object
codebase=*url*	Sets the base URL for the object; helps resolve relative references
codetype=*type*	Identifies the content type of the data in the object
data=*url*	Identifies the location of the object's data
declare	Indicates the object will be declared only, not installed in the page
height=*value*	Sets the height of the object to a value in pixels
name=*text*	Assigns a control name to the object for use in forms
standby=*text*	Defines the message to display while the object loads
tabindex=*value*	Specifies the tab order between elements, with 1 as the first element
type=*type*	Specifies the content or media type of the object
usemap=*url*	Associates an imagemap as defined by the <map> element
width=*value*	Sets the width of the object to a value in pixels
<ol>....</ol>	Defines an ordered list that contains numbered list item elements (<li>)
type=*option*	Sets or resets the numbering format for the list; options include: A=capital letters, a=lowercase letters, I=capital Roman numerals, i=lowercase Roman numerals, or **1**=Arabic numerals
<option>....</option>	Defines individual options in a selection list, as defined by <select> element
label=*text*	Provides a shorter label for the option than that specified in its content
selected	Sets the option to be the default or the selected option in a list
value=*value*	Sets a value returned to the server when the user selects the option
disabled	Disables the option items
<p>....</p>	Delimits a paragraph; automatically inserts a blank line between text
align=*position*	Aligns text within the paragraph (left, center, right)
<param>....</param>	Passes a parameter to an object or applet, as defined by <object> or <applet> element
id=*text*	Assigns an identifier to the element
name=*text*	Defines the name of the parameter required by an object
type=*type*	Specifies the content or media type of the object
value=*data*	Sets the value of the parameter
valuetype=*data*	Identifies the type of parameter used in the value attribute (data, ref, object)
<pre>....</pre>	Preserves the original format of the enclosed text; keeps line breaks and spacing the same as the original
No attributes	

Table A-1 HTML Tags and Attributes (continued)

HTML TAG AND ATTRIBUTES	DESCRIPTION
<q>....</q>	Sets enclosed text as a short quotation
lang=*option*	Defines the language in which the quotation will display
<samp>....</samp>	Sets enclosed text to display as sample output from a computer program or script; usually displays in a monospace font
No attributes	
<script>....</script>	Inserts a client-side script into an HTML document
defer	Indicates that the browser should defer executing the script
src=*url*	Identifies the location of an external script
type=*mime-type*	Indicates the data or media type of the script language (e.g., text/javascript for JavaScript commands)
<select>....</select>	Defines a form control to create a multiple-choice menu or scrolling list; encloses a set of <option> tags to define one or more options
name=*text*	Assigns a name to the selection list
multiple	Sets the list to allow multiple selections
size=*value*	Sets the number of visible options in the list
disabled	Disables the selection list
tabindex=*value*	Specifies the tab order between list items, with 1 as the first element
<small>....</small>	Sets enclosed text to display in a smaller typeface
No attributes	
<span>....</span>	Creates a user-defined container to add inline structure to the HTML document
No attributes	
<strong>....</strong>	Sets enclosed text to display with strong emphasis; usually displayed as bold text
No attributes	
<style>....</style>	Encloses embedded style sheet rules for use in the HTML document
media=*data*	Identifies the intended medium of the style (**screen**, tty, tv, projection, handheld, print, braille, aural, all)
title=*data*	Indicates the title of the style sheet
type=*data*	Specifies the content or media type of the style language (e.g., text/css for linked style sheets)
<sub>....</sub>	Sets enclosed text to display in subscript
No attributes	
<sup>....</sup>	Sets enclosed text to display in superscript
No attributes	
<table>....</table>	Marks the start and end of a table
align=*position*	Aligns the table text (left, right, center, justify, char)
border=*value*	Sets the border around a table to a value in pixels
cellpadding=*value*	Sets padding around each cell's contents to a value in pixels
cellspacing=*value*	Sets spacing between cells to a value in pixels
summary=*text*	Provides a summary of the table's purpose and structure
width=*value or %*	Sets table width in pixels or a percentage of the window

Table A-1 HTML Tags and Attributes

HTML TAG AND ATTRIBUTES	DESCRIPTION
\<table\>....\</table\> *(continued)*	
frame=*option*	Defines which parts of the outer border (frame) to display (void, above, below, hsides, lhs, rhs, vsides, box, border)
rules=*option*	Specifies which inner borders are to display between the table cells (none, groups, rows, cols, all)
\<tbody\>....\</tbody\>	Defines a groups of rows in a table body
align=*option*	Aligns text (left, center, right, justify, char)
char=*character*	Specifies a character on which to align column values (e.g., a period is used to align monetary values)
charoff=*value*	Specifies a number of characters to offset data aligned with the character specified in the char property
valign=*position*	Sets vertical alignment of cells in a group (top, middle, bottom, baseline)
\<td\>....\</td\>	Defines a data cell in a table; contents are left-aligned and normal text by default
bgcolor=*color*	Defines the background color for the cell
colspan=*value*	Defines the number of adjacent columns spanned by the cell
rowspan=*value*	Defines the number of adjacent rows spanned by the cell
width=*n* or %	Sets the width of the table in either pixels or a percentage of the whole table width
headers=*idrefs*	Defines the list of header cells for the current cell
abbr=*text*	Provides an abbreviated version of the cell's contents that browsers can use if space is limited
scope=*option*	Specifies cells for which the element defines header cells (row, col, rowgroup, colgroup)
align=*position*	Specifies horizontal alignment (left, center, right, justify, char)
char=*character*	Specifies a character on which to align column values (e.g., a period is used to align monetary values)
charoff=*value*	Specifies a number of characters to offset data aligned with the character specified in the char property
valign=*position*	Sets vertical alignment of cells in the group (top, middle, bottom, baseline)
\<textarea\>....\</textarea\>	Creates a multiline text input area within a form
cols=*value*	Defines the number of columns in the text input area
name=*data*	Assigns a name to the text area
rows=*value*	Defines the number of rows in the text input area
disabled	Disables the element
readonly	Prevents the user from editing content in the text area
tabindex=*value*	Specifies the tab order between elements, with 1 as the first element
\<tfoot\>....\</tfoot\>	Identifies and groups rows into a table footer
align=*position*	Specifies horizontal alignment (left, center, right, justify, char)
char=*character*	Specifies a character on which to align column values (e.g., a period is used to align monetary values)
charoff=*value*	Specifies a number of characters to offset data aligned with the character specified in the char property
valign=*position*	Sets vertical alignment of cells in a group (top, middle, bottom, baseline)

Table A-1 HTML Tags and Attributes (continued)

HTML TAG AND ATTRIBUTES	DESCRIPTION
\<th\>....\</th\>	Defines a table header cell; contents are bold and center-aligned by default
bgcolor=*color*	Defines the background color for the cell
colspan=*value*	Defines the number of adjacent columns spanned by the cell
rowspan=*value*	Defines the number of adjacent rows spanned by the cell
width=*n* or *%*	Sets the width of the table in either pixels or a percentage of the whole table width
\<thead\>....\</thead\>	Identifies and groups rows into a table header
align=*position*	Specifies horizontal alignment (left, center, right, justify, char)
char=*character*	Specifies a character on which to align column values (e.g., a period is used to align monetary values)
charoff=*value*	Specifies a number of characters to offset data aligned with the character specified in the char property
valign=*position*	Sets vertical alignment of cells in a group (top, middle, bottom, baseline)
\<title\>....\</title\>	Defines the title for the HTML document; always should be used
No attributes	
\<tr\>....\</tr\>	Defines a row of cells within a table
bgcolor=*color*	Defines the background color for the cell
align=*position*	Specifies horizontal alignment (left, center, right, justify, char)
char=*character*	Specifies a character on which to align column values (e.g., a period is used to align monetary values)
charoff=*value*	Specifies a number of characters to offset data aligned with the character specified in the char property
valign=*position*	Sets vertical alignment of cells in a group (top, middle, bottom, baseline)
\<tt\>....\</tt\>	Formats the enclosed text in teletype- or computer-style monospace font
No attributes	
\<u\>....\</u\> *	Sets enclosed text to display with an underline
No attributes	
\<ul\>....\</ul\>	Defines an unnumbered list that contains bulleted list item elements (\<li\>)
type=*option*	Sets or resets the bullet format for the list; options include: circle, **disc**, square
\<var\>....\</var\>	Indicates the enclosed text is a variable's name; used to mark up variables or program arguments
No attributes	

Appendix B

Browser-Safe Color Palette

Browser-Safe Colors

Three hardware components help to deliver color to a computer user: the processor, the video card, and the monitor. Because of the wide variety of components that exist, the color quality that users see varies greatly. The software on a user's computer, specifically the Web browser, also affects the way that color is displayed on a monitor. For Web developers, it is the browser that limits color significantly. It is very difficult, if not impossible, to plan for all possible color variations created by a Web browser. Using browser-safe colors allows for the browser variations, but limits the number of colors used on the Web page.

A total of 216 browser-safe colors display well on different monitors, operating systems, and browsers — including both Windows and Mac OS operating systems and Internet Explorer and Netscape Navigator browsers. When using color on your Web site, keep in mind that using only the 216 browser-safe colors can be very restrictive, especially for the approximately ten percent of Web visitors who have 256-color monitors. On those monitors, only the browser-safe colors will display. If you decide to use a non-browser-safe color, the visitor's browser will try to create the color by combining (a process called dithering) any number of the 216 acceptable colors. The resulting color could be slightly different from the color you had intended.

For a complete list of the 216 browser-safe colors, see Table B-1 on the next page or visit the Shelly Cashman Series HTML Web page (scsite.com/html3e) and click Color Chart. Links to other Web sites with information about browser-safe colors also are available.

Table B-1 Browser-Safe Colors

#ffffff	#ffffcc	#ffff99	#ffff66	#ffff33	#ffff00
#ffccff	#ffcccc	#ffcc99	#ffcc66	#ffcc33	#ffcc00
#ff99ff	#ff99cc	#ff9999	#ff9966	#ff9933	#ff9900
#ff66ff	#ff66cc	#ff6699	#ff6666	#ff6633	#ff6600
#ff33ff	#ff33cc	#ff3399	#ff3366	#ff3333	#ff3300
#ff00ff	#ff00cc	#ff0099	#ff0066	#ff0033	#ff0000
#ccffff	#ccffcc	#ccff99	#ccff66	#ccff33	#ccff00
#ccccff	#cccccc	#cccc99	#cccc66	#cccc33	#cccc00
#cc99ff	#cc99cc	#cc9999	#cc9966	#cc9933	#cc9900
#cc66ff	#cc66cc	#cc6699	#cc6666	#cc6633	#cc6600
#cc33ff	#cc33cc	#cc3399	#cc3366	#cc3333	#cc3300
#cc00ff	#cc00cc	#cc0099	#cc0066	#cc0033	#cc0000
#99ffff	#99ffcc	#99ff99	#99ff66	#99ff33	#99ff00
#99ccff	#99cccc	#99cc99	#99cc66	#99cc33	#99cc00
#9999ff	#9999cc	#999999	#999966	#999933	#999900
#9966ff	#9966cc	#996699	#996666	#996633	#996600
#9933ff	#9933cc	#993399	#993366	#993333	#993300
#9900ff	#9900cc	#990099	#990066	#990033	#990000
#66ffff	#66ffcc	#66ff99	#66ff66	#66ff33	#66ff00
#66ccff	#66cccc	#66cc99	#66cc66	#66cc33	#66cc00
#6699ff	#6699cc	#669999	#669966	#669933	#669900
#6666ff	#6666cc	#666699	#666666	#666633	#666600
#6633ff	#6633cc	#663399	#663366	#663333	#663300
#6600ff	#6600cc	#660099	#660066	#660033	#660000
#33ffff	#33ffcc	#33ff99	#33ff66	#33ff33	#33ff00
#33ccff	#33cccc	#33cc99	#33cc66	#33cc33	#33cc00
#3399ff	#3399cc	#339999	#339966	#339933	#339900
#3366ff	#3366cc	#336699	#336666	#336633	#336600
#3333ff	#3333cc	#333399	#333366	#333333	#333300
#3300ff	#3300cc	#330099	#330066	#330033	#330000
#00ffff	#00ffcc	#00ff99	#00ff66	#00ff33	#00ff00
#00ccff	#00cccc	#00cc99	#00cc66	#00cc33	#00cc00
#0099ff	#0099cc	#009999	#009966	#009933	#009900
#0066ff	#0066cc	#006699	#006666	#006633	#006600
#0033ff	#0033cc	#003399	#003366	#003333	#003300
#0000ff	#0000cc	#000099	#000066	#000033	#000000

Index